FENG SHUI & DESTINY FOR MANAGERS

RAYMOND LO

TIMES BOOKS INTERNATIONAL
Singapore • Kuala Lumpur

Published by Times Books International
an imprint of Times Editions Pte Ltd
Times Centre
1 New Industrial Road
Singapore 1953

Times Subang
Lot 46, Subang Hi-Tech Industrial Park
Batu Tiga
40000 Shah Alam
Selangor Darul Ehsan
Malaysia

Printed in Singapore

ISBN 981 204 620 8

Acknowledgements

I would like to thank everyone who supported and encouraged me during the writing of this book, especially my parents, my wife Maureen, my teacher Master Suen, my publisher Times Editions and my students who listened so patiently and generously shared their own knowledge. I am fully indebted to them for providing me with the drive to continue my research into the outer frontiers of Chinese metaphysics.

CONTENTS

Appendices

PREFACE

Dealing with uncertainties and risks is the basic responsibility of every manager in the highly competitive business world. There are many management tools designed to tackle risks and to make forecasts and projections but few can truly include the essential factors of chance and luck which are just unknown quantities at the planning stage. Even the most brilliant economists and managers can never be right all the time. Unforeseeable events, such as the weather, natural disasters, political changes and other events classified as *force majeur*, may upset forecasts based on experience and statistical tools. This is where Chinese metaphysics can play an important role.

In the Asian business community, the application of Chinese metaphysical tools is widespread. Many firms consult a *feng shui* expert for their office decoration and design. Often, they also use Chinese metaphysical means to select auspicious dates for important events. Many successful managers consult fortune-tellers when making important decisions, such as starting a risky project, changing jobs or resolving human conflict in the business environment.

However, like engaging any other consultant, managers still need to equip themselves with some understanding of the subject, so that they can at least determine whether the advice offered by experts is convincing or practical. Good Chinese metaphysical advice is not easy to obtain and there is considerable misunderstanding and exaggeration about the subject. Some fortune-tellers, lacking a strong theoretical foundation, may not fully appreciate a manager's problem and give advice that is neither practical nor relevant.

The best remedy then for a modern manager is to equip himself with some basic knowledge about Chinese metaphysics, so that he can make optimum use of this technique in his business.

This book has been written to meet the needs of managers who are open to using unconventional tools in their decision making. It introduces a wide range of basic techniques in Chinese metaphysics, including *feng shui*, the Four Pillars of Destiny and the I Ching Oracle, that managers can apply to their business environment as an alternative means to handling risks and uncertainties.

As the focus is on business management, I have included many examples on solving daily management problems, such as project risk and profitability analysis, staff selection, bidding for a project, choosing business partners, office decoration and design and selecting a good logo. For readers who are not in the business field, this book can still serve as a text for learning practical *feng shui* and destiny techniques.

The subject of Chinese metaphysics is so vast that it is impossible to convey adequate information in a slim volume as this but I have tried to make this book as self-sufficient as possible by adding appendices showing step-by-step practical processes. Hence this book can also be used as a do-it-yourself guide for practising *feng shui* and destiny analysis methods. My other writings can also be used as supplementary tools if readers wish to enhance their understanding of the methods introduced here.

What Is Destiny?

The Cantonese have an interesting saying. When discussing the factors that affect one's quality of life, they say "Destiny comes first, luck, second and *feng shui*, third."

I therefore begin this book with a thorough discussion on destiny. By destiny, we usually refer to matters which are determined by some higher power and are beyond our freewill and control. A common element of destiny is the inborn qualities of a person. We are all born with different intelligence, temperament, aptitudes, physique and character, qualities which each of us carries to this world at the moment of birth. These factors will have a significant impact on our growth and path in life, and most of them cannot be modified, even by education or by the environment in which a person is brought up. These inborn factors can be regarded as the components of a person. It is the variations in these components that make people so different from one another.

Destiny, therefore, can be viewed as the fundamental composition of each individual as well as the variation in such composition. It does not refer to the biological structure of the body, which is more or less similar. It should be appreciated in a broader sense, embracing every aspect of a person's life, including his character, potential, position in our complex society, relationships with other people and even matters as abstract as human fortune, luck and fate. To explain this inborn composition of an individual, the Chinese have a unique system of cosmology which can be employed to define and explain destiny. This system is known as the Theory of the Five Basic Elements.

Theory Of The Five Basic Elements

The origin of the theory is lost in ancient Chinese history, but the mention and use of this philosophy can be found as far back as the period of the warring states immediately preceding the Chin Dynasty, around 240 B.C. It is believed that the five elements—metal, wood, water, fire and earth—are the fundamental forces, or energies, in the universe. Everything in the universe, both material and abstract, results from the interaction of these five elements. The elements can be applied to every aspect of life. For example, spring is considered a season of wood; the music note "la" is a sound of the water element; the colour white is the colour of metal whereas black is the colour of water; south is the direction of fire; and the human stomach is an organ of the earth element. Even the Chin Dynasty is considered a dynasty of the water element, and the first emperor was known to have worn black robes and to have used black flags.

Although the five basic elements are named after objects commonly found on earth, they should not be viewed as physical objects. They are, in fact, five kinds of invisible, interacting energies which can be regarded as the basic driving forces in the cosmos. However, each of these forces do carry the characteristics of the physical symbol. For example, the wood element prospers in spring, is green in colour and controls earth because its roots can grow deep into the ground. Therefore, it may be convenient to understand these forces according to their physical names.

As man is merely a small object in the universe, we are also governed by and subject to the rules and order of the universe. Just as everything in the universe is composed of the five basic elements, we are no exception and the composition of human destiny is also a composition of the five basic elements. The differences in each person's destiny can be revealed by variations in the composition of the five elements.

Before we delve deeper into the subject of interpreting human destiny by the theory of the five elements, let us first examine the two basic relationships among the elements.

Interactions Of The Basic Elements

The five basic forces in the universe are not static. They are constantly interacting with each other, and it is believed that all motions and changes in the universe, resulting in men, matter and events, are caused and affected by the interactions of the five basic elements. However, the universe is not chaotic. The elements interact with one another according to some fundamental rules.

These rules are the Cycle of Birth and the Cycle of Destruction. The two cycles are illustrated by Figure 1.

Fig. 1 The Cycle of Birth and The Cycle of Destruction

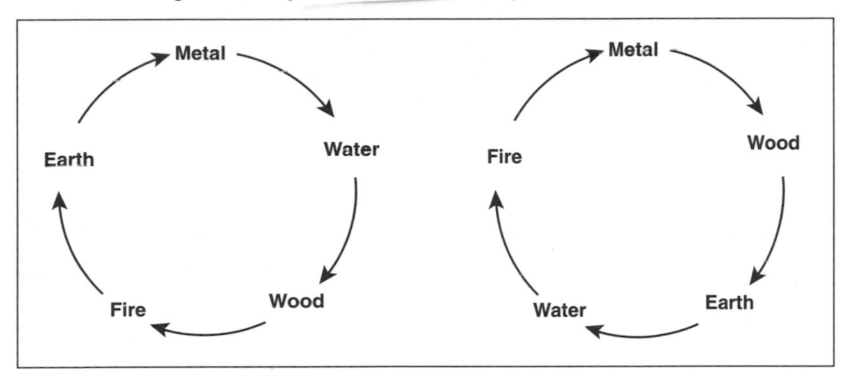

The Cycle of Birth shows that an element can give birth, or provide support to another, in a cyclical manner. This is a mother-and-child, harmonious relationship. On the other hand, the Cycle of Destruction shows a conflicting relationship, such that an element also destroys, controls or suppresses another.

The world comes alive with the interaction of the five basic forces and it is through the understanding of this order, or Tao, that the ancient Chinese derived considerable knowledge about the universe. It is not only time, space and nature that can be explained in terms of the five elements. The theory even provides the bridge between man and the universe. It was through the theory of the five basic elements that the Chinese developed a profound system of human destiny analysis which is able to reveal and forecast the impact of the universe on each individual through the passage of time.

It may seem incredible to talk about generalising the complicated universe and human society into five basic elements. Yet, the same simple theory is the foundation of Chinese herbal medicine and acupuncture. These medical skills have served the Chinese for thousands of years and their efficacy in treating many illnesses has now become the focus of attention of Western medical experts.

Chinese medicine also assigns a basic element to each of the vital organs. For instance, the fire element symbolises the heart, the metal element symbolises the lung, the wood element represents the liver and the water element represents the kidney. A person should be in good health if all five organs, represented by the five elements, are in a balanced and harmonious state and interact with one another according to the cycles of birth and destruction. On the other hand, if an element grows excessively strong or weak, the balance will be upset and illness will occur. For example, if the kidney is weak, water, a symbol of the kidney, will not be able to keep fire under control. The result will be illness related to the heart, such as irregular heartbeat or high blood pressure, as fire symbolises the heart and blood. The remedy is to use herbal medicine or acupuncture, to regain the body balance.

The interaction of the five basic elements not only governs the functions of our internal organs, but also constitutes our life and destiny. As such grand rules govern the entire universe, it is only logical to deduce that man should also be subject to the same order. This knowledge linking man directly to the universal order has not only been applied very successfully in Chinese medicine, but also forms the basic framework of a profound system of human destiny analysis, popularly known as the Four Pillars of Destiny.

In many systems of fortune-telling around the world, the moment of birth is invariably taken as the birth mark and the starting point of life, and all predictions about the future life pattern of a child is based on it. In other words, the moment of birth is our identity and cosmic code or blueprint. It provides each individual with a unique identification through which the composition of an individual's fortune, destiny and future life pattern can be deciphered. Western astrology utilises the birth data to draw up a horoscope which reflects the position of the planets in the solar system, and uses these star charts to reveal destiny.

In China, the method is more handy. It is only necessary to express the birth data as a composition of the five elements and our destiny can be fully revealed by interpreting the strengths and weaknesses of these elements and how they interact with one another. As four pieces of information are required to form such a code of destiny, namely the birth year, month, day and hour, the art is called the Four Pillars of Destiny, with each piece of information called a pillar.

Before we get down to understanding how the Four Pillars of Destiny drawn up from our birth data can reflect the composition of destiny, let me briefly explain the background and mechanism of the Chinese calendar.

Understanding The Chinese Calendar

The Chinese have adopted two different calendar systems. The one used by laymen is the lunar calendar, which divides a year into 12 months, based on the motion of the moon as it orbits the earth. There is another calendar which is not only used to count the days, but is also used for farming and fortune-telling. This is a solar calendar which the Chinese call the Hsia calendar, as it has been on record since the Hsia Dynasty about 4,000 years ago.

The main difference between the Hsia calendar and the lunar calendar is that the former is a solar calendar, meaning that the year is counted according to the motion of the earth round the sun, and each month is divided according to the position of the sun relative to the earth. The Hsia calendar is unique because it is closely related to the five basic elements. Each year, month and day on this calendar is expressed in terms of two Chinese characters, each representing one of the five basic elements. For example, the year 1993 is expressed in the Hsia calendar by the two Chinese characters "癸酉". The first character represents the water element while the second represents metal. Any moment of time can be expressed in terms of the elements. By translating a moment of time—year, month, day and hour—into the Hsia calendar format, we immediately obtain eight Chinese characters representing eight elements prevailing at that time.

Likewise, a person's birth year, month, day and hour can be expressed in a set of Four Pillars containing eight elements. Let me illustrate this with an example. Say, we have a baby boy born at the hour 2000 on 9 January in the year 1913. By looking up a book called *The Thousand Year Calendar*, we can translate this time into the Hsia calendar format. The Chinese characters representing this moment of time are as follows:

A sample Four Pillars of Destiny for a boy born at 2000 hours, 9 January 1913

Hour	Day	Month	Year
丙	庚	癸	壬
戌	寅	丑	子

Readers can see that the moment of birth—hour, day, month and year—can be expressed in terms of eight Chinese characters. The Chinese characters on top are called the heavenly stems and the characters below are the earthly branches. There are altogether 10 heavenly stems and 12 earthly branches, and these 22 Chinese characters form the basis of the Hsia calendar. By presenting the birth data in this format, we see that each Chinese character, in fact, symbolises an element. Therefore we can immediately translate the eight Chinese characters into elements according to the following table:

Heavenly Stems		**Earthly Branches**	
甲	Yang wood	子	Water (Mouse)
乙	Yin wood	丑	Earth (Ox)
丙	Yang fire	寅	Wood (Tiger)
丁	Yin fire	卯	Wood (Rabbit)
戊	Yang earth	辰	Earth (Dragon)
己	Yin earth	巳	Fire (Snake)
庚	Yang metal	午	Fire (Horse)
辛	Yin metal	未	Earth (Ram)
壬	Yang water	申	Metal (Monkey)
癸	Yin water	酉	Metal (Rooster)
		戌	Earth (Dog)
		亥	Water (Pig)

As the Hsia calendar provides us with information about the influence of the five basic elements prevailing at any moment of time, a set of birth data, presented in the Hsia calendar format of heavenly stems and earthly branches, actually tells us the elemental influence at the moment of birth. It is believed to be the representation of the cosmic components of a person at birth. Once we know the components of the five elements in our lives, the rules governing the interaction of these elements and the pattern of change of the elements through time, we can derive and predict our future pattern of life. This method of deriving destiny by elemental influence is the art of Chinese fortune-telling called the Four Pillars of Destiny. It is called the four pillars because our destiny is composed of four pieces of information about time—year, month, day and hour—and each piece constitutes a pillar containing two elements, one on the heavenly stem, the other on the earthly branch.

Returning to the sample birth data shown earlier, let us now look up the table and translate the Chinese characters into the five basic elements:

The Four Pillars of Destiny expressed in elements

Hour	Day	Month	Year
丙 Fire	庚 Metal	癸 Water	壬 Water
戌 Earth	寅 Wood	丑 Earth	子 Water

We can see that the boy born at about 2000 hours on 9 January 1913 is composed of a bundle of elements, with three water, one wood, one fire, one metal and two earth. This is the composition of the life and destiny of a man.

Interpreting Destiny

Throughout Chinese history, there were many great scholars and sages who devoted their lives to developing tools to interpret human destiny. One of the most famous of these men was Tsu Ping, who lived around 800 A.D. Tsu Ping established some important ground rules, making it easier to interpret destiny by examining the elements reflected in a set of birth data. The first step, according to Tsu Ping, is to establish the self from the bundle of elements. The heavenly stem of the day pillar always represents the self, while the remaining seven elements are considered as the surrounding, relatives and friends. In our example, as the heavenly stem of the day pillar is occupied by the metal element, the person is therefore a metal man.

After establishing the element of the self, the next step is to see the disposition of the self amongst the other seven elements. The Chinese believe in the principle of balance and harmony in the universe. Any excessiveness, whether weakness or strength, is considered as disharmony and means misfortune in destiny. As such, after establishing the self element, we need to evaluate how strong or weak the self is amongst the other seven elements.

To do this, two aspects need to be examined. One is the quantity of the self element. The other more essential aspect is the seasonal strength of the element, as each element is believed to have a seasonal cycle from birth to death. The following table shows such a seasonal cycle:

	Metal	Wood	Water	Fire
Spring	die	prosper	weak	born
Summer	born	weak	die	prosper
Autumn	prosper	die	born	weak
Winter	weak	born	prosper	die

According to the table, metal is most prosperous in autumn, wood in spring, water is strongest in winter while fire reaches its peak of prosperity in summer. Note that there is no earth element in the table as earth is considered the basic element to all others and is prosperous in the third month of each season.

These seasonal changes in the cycle of the five elements have been incorporated into the Chinese Hsia calendar system. The 12 months of a year are defined by the different positions of the sun relative to the earth on the imaginary circle called the ecliptic. The year commences from the first day of spring which normally falls on 4 or 5 February in the Western calendar, and ends on the last day of winter when the earth completes the circle. The 12 months are formed by dividing the ecliptic into 12 portions and naming them according to the 12 earthly branches. The year which starts around 4 February is expressed by the earthly branch " 寅 ", symbolising the wood element. The relationship between the Hsia calendar and the Western calendar is listed out in the following table:

Hsia Months		Element	Season	Western Months
1	寅	Wood	Spring	4, 5 Feb – 5, 6 Mar
2	卯	Wood	Spring	5, 6 Mar – 4, 5 Apr
3	辰	Earth	Spring	4, 5 Apr – 5, 6 May
4	巳	Fire	Summer	5, 6 May – 5, 6 June
5	午	Fire	Summer	5, 6 June – 7, 8 July
6	未	Earth	Summer	7, 8 July – 7, 8 Aug
7	申	Metal	Autumn	7, 8 Aug – 7, 8 Sep
8	酉	Metal	Autumn	7, 8 Sep – 8, 9 Oct
9	戌	Earth	Autumn	8, 9 Oct – 7, 8 Nov
10	亥	Water	Winter	7, 8 Nov – 7, 8 Dec
11	子	Water	Winter	7, 8 Dec – 5, 6 Jan
12	丑	Earth	Winter	5, 6 Jan – 4, 5 Feb

In the table, we can observe that the Chinese calendar also incorporates the influence of the five basic elements in each month. Spring is considered a month when plants will prosper, so the first two months of spring are symbolised by earthly branches representing the wood element. Summer is a hot season in the northern hemisphere and is represented by the fire earthly branches. Readers can also see that every third month of each season is symbolised by an earth element, since earth is basic to all other elements and its influence prevails throughout the year.

Besides the year, month and day, the Hsia calendar also expresses the 24 hours of a day in terms of the elements represented by the heavenly stems and earthly branches. As there are only 12 earthly branches, the Chinese have grouped two hours into one and formed a system which has only 12 hours. The following table shows the 12 hour system in the Hsia calendar:

Hsia Hours		Animal	Element	Western Time
1	子	Rat	Water	2300 – 0100
2	丑	Ox	Earth	0100 – 0300
3	寅	Tiger	Wood	0300 – 0500
4	卯	Rabbit	Wood	0500 – 0700
5	辰	Dragon	Earth	0700 – 0900
6	巳	Snake	Fire	0900 – 1100
7	午	Horse	Fire	1100 – 1300
8	未	Goat	Earth	1300 – 1500
9	申	Monkey	Metal	1500 – 1700
10	酉	Rooster	Metal	1700 – 1900
11	戌	Dog	Earth	1900 – 2100
12	亥	Pig	Water	2100 – 2300

The Hsia calendar enables us to express any moment of time in terms of elements through the system of heavenly stems and earthly branches. We can then see what elemental influence the universe exerts on human fortune at any time, in the past or the future, and go on to predict the future by evaluating the impact of these elemental forces on our birth data.

Knowing the relation between the Chinese calendar system and the cycle of prosperity of the five basic elements, we can now examine the strength of the self in a set of Four Pillars. For example, if the element representing the self is fire, and this fire is born in winter, we can see, from the table, that since fire dies in winter, the fire is weak. On the other hand, if this fire person is born in the summer when fire is most prosperous, then the fire person is considered strong fire. However fire born in winter should not automatically be taken as weak fire. There are other factors to consider—one of which is the quantity factor, that is, the number of supportive elements in the set of four pillars. Taking fire as an example again, if the fire is born in winter, but in the set of four pillars, there are many other fire and wood elements which are both supportive of such fire, then the fire self will be strengthened. We therefore have to exercise our judgement before deciding whether the self is strong or weak.

After making a decision on the strength or weakness of the self element, the third step is to find the favourable and unfavourable elements to the self. This is a balancing step and is essential in forecasting the fortune of a person. The entire philosophy of the Four Pillars of Destiny is one of balance and harmony. Even the name of the man who reorganised the art into its present form, Tsu Ping, carries the meaning "balancing the water". The point is that the element representing the self cannot be excessively strong or weak. In both cases, it means misfortune in life.

If the self is excessively strong, it is necessary to suppress or release its excessive strength. This can be achieved with elements which can suppress or release its energy. On the other hand, if the self element is too weak, it is necessary to support it with other elements which will give birth to or provide support to the self. For example, if the self is fire and the fire is very strong, the favourable elements can be water, metal and earth. Water will suppress the strong fire while metal and earth will also help to exhaust the excessive fire energy, as the cycles of birth and destruction show us that fire conquers metal and also gives birth to earth. By the act of conquering or giving birth to other elements, the strength of fire can be weakened. Similarly, if the fire is too weak, it is necessary to give it the support of more wood and fire, as wood is the mother of fire according to the cycle of birth, while other fire elements are also helpful colleagues.

The essence is that if the self is too strong or too weak, it is unhealthy. The self has to be given medicine in the form of other elements to improve the fortune. Favourable elements will help bring about balance and harmony. Elements which intensify the imbalance are considered unfavourable elements.

As the Chinese Hsia calendar tells us what elemental influences we can expect at any moment of time, we can assess our fortune at that particular moment merely by observing if the elemental influences are favourable or unfavourable. If a person is a weak fire, his favourable elements are wood and fire, and his unfavourable elements, water and metal. For the year 1993, the Hsia calendar tells us that the prevailing influence is metal and water. We can then predict that a weak fire person will encounter a year of misfortune in 1993. By this method the Four Pillars of Destiny is able to reflect the life pattern of each individual —its ups and downs, successes and failures.

The Rise And Fall Of Richard Nixon

Let me demonstrate with an example. The sample set of Pillars of Destiny for the boy born on 9 January 1913 that we used earlier, in fact, belongs to former United States President Richard Nixon.

President Nixon was born in a day of metal in winter. He is thus a metal person. As water is most prosperous in winter, and there are three prominent water elements in his set of Four Pillars, water appears to be the most powerful element in this configuration. According to the cycle of birth, water is generated by metal. As the strong water element will exhaust the metal energy, President Nixon can be regarded as a weak metal person. To attain balance, he needs the earth element to provide nourishment and support to the metal. The fire element is also useful as it supports the earth, as well as injects warmth to the destiny. Therefore, earth and fire are his favourable elements. On the other hand, water and wood, being adversaries of fire and earth, in accordance with the cycle of destruction, are unfavourable elements.

Having established his favourable and unfavourable elements, let us now examine some events in President Nixon's life to see if earth and fire brought him any good luck and if water and wood brought him misfortunes. President Nixon first ran for the presidency in 1960 but was defeated

by President John F. Kennedy. The year 1960 was a year of strong water (庚子), which is an unfavourable element to President Nixon. However, he eventually succeeded in his second attempt and became President in 1968 (戊申), a year of the favourable earth element. Unfortunately, in the year 1972 (壬子), another year of strong water influence, President Nixon encountered the Watergate incident which caused his eventual impeachment by Congress in 1974 (甲子), a year of the unfavourable wood element. From this brief account of President Nixon's political ups and downs, it is easy to see how changes in the influence of the five basic elements can bring about a change of fortune to the individual. If we can understand such patterns of change of the five elements, we can then use these patterns to forecast our future and help us make business decisions.

Are You The Business Type?

In the previous chapter, I briefly introduced the mechanisms behind the use of the Four Pillars of Destiny to predict our life patterns. This metaphysical means of forecasting is especially useful if we wish to decide whether to enter a high-risk business venture. The Four Pillars of Destiny can reveal our up and down cycles in life. If destiny indicates that a down cycle is immediately ahead, it is best to refrain from risky ventures. On the other hand, if an up cycle of personal prosperity is anticipated, you can pursue the venture with greater confidence.

The last chapter only revealed a general outline of the Four Pillars of Destiny. Besides reflecting the cyclical life pattern of a person, this fascinating technique can also reveal other aspects of life in detail. This is achieved through observing the interrelationships among the five basic elements, with the self as the centre for reference and comparison. In traditional Chinese society, the major aspects of life include the following areas: power, authority, status, wealth, education, intelligence, aspirations, colleagues and partnerships. I believe these aspects also encompass the wide scope of modern business life. In this chapter, I will show you how these aspects of life can be evaluated from our birth data.

It is important to understand our potential and aptitudes before we enter any kind of business venture. Man is not born equal. Different persons possess different potential and aptitudes. Some of us are born businessmen with a strong aptitude for finance and running our own business. Others are more interested in power and status and are better working as government officials or administrators. There are still others who are more suited to the academic world or the arts.

In our extremely competitive society, it is essential to choose a career which suits our aptitude and interests. It is a sheer wastage of effort and time to take up a career which does not match our character. If, for example, a person who dislikes meeting people takes up a sales job, I believe no matter how hard he tries, his chances of success is considerably less than another person who enjoys talking to people. We arc better off pursuing a career which matches our inborn potential and interests. And the Four Pillars of Destiny is a tool which can help us understand our potential.

Before getting into any career, you need to first understand yourself by examining your own Four Pillars of Destiny. This is again done through examining the interrelationship among the five basic elements, according to the cycles of birth and destruction. Since the fundamental goal of doing business is financial reward, the first aspect we will examine is wealth. The basic question you need to ask yourself is, do you have the aptitude to run a business? In other words, are you destined to be businessman?

If we have a set of birth data expressed in terms of the Four Pillars of Destiny, the first step is to establish what the self is. This can be easily determined, as by definition, the self is the element occupying the heavenly stem of the day pillar. In our example of President Nixon in the last chapter, the self is symbolised by the metal element.

The next step is to determine which is the element of wealth in the set of four pillars. The philosophy is that wealth is an object conquered by the self. So logically, it is represented by the element which is conquered by the self, according to the cycle of destruction. In the case of President Nixon, a metal man, the element conquered by metal is wood. Hence wood is the element symbolising wealth in his destiny. Using this method, we can find the element of wealth in any set of pillars of destiny.

Hong Kong Tycoon Li Ka-shing

After finding the element symbolising wealth in our destiny, the next step is to evaluate the strength of these elements. If there are many wealth elements, obviously money will feature quite strongly in the person's life. The following set of Four Pillars of Destiny is an example:

The Pillars of Destiny of Li Ka-shing (13/6/1928)

Hour	Day	Month	Year
?	甲 Wood	戊 Earth	戊 Earth
?	申 Metal	午 Fire	辰 Earth

These pillars of destiny belong to Hong Kong property tycoon and billionaire Mr. Li Ka-shing—one of the richest men in the world. Applying the same method, we discover that Mr. Li is a wood person. As wood conquers earth, the earth element symbolises wealth in his destiny. The numerous earth elements in his destiny clearly show that he is a very wealthy person and that his wealth is acquired mainly from properties—the earth element.

Wealth is certainly not the only important aspect of life. There are many other areas which are equally—perhaps even more—important than riches. I will now give some brief guidelines on how to read other aspects of life from the Four Pillars of Destiny. The following list shows how various aspects of life can be interpreted from destiny by comparing the relationship between the self and the other elements:

- Wealth—the element conquered by the self. If the self is wood, wood conquers earth. Earth is then wealth to a wood person.
- Power and status—the element that conquers the self. If the self is wood, then power and status is represented by metal, as metal conquers wood.
- Resources and education—the element that gives birth to the self is resources and education. For example, water is the element symbolising resources and education to a person whose day pillar is wood as water gives birth to wood.
- Intelligence and aspirations—the element that is given birth by the self is one's intelligence and aspirations, as it is something a person produces, creates and presents to the world. In the case of a wood person, the fire element is a symbol of his intelligence as wood generates fire.
- Colleagues or competitors—the element that is same as the self represents colleagues or competitors. If the self is wood, then other wood he encounters in his four pillars are his colleagues, friends or competitors, depending on whether they are favourable or unfavourable.

Appendix 4 provides more details about finding various aspects of life and human relationships from our pillars of destiny.

By understanding the relationship between the different elements in a set of Four Pillars of Destiny, it is not difficult to see which element is most prominent and casts the strongest influence on a person. Looking at the example of Mr. Li Ka-shing, the element of earth, representing his wealth, is obviously most prominent. His life is surrounded by wealth, especially wealth related to earth—his property business. We can also observe that the element representing power and status—metal in his case—only occupies a single position. Therefore, he is not a politician and wealth, not power, is his destiny in life.

We can also find out our inborn potential from our birth data and lessen considerably the chances of choosing a wrong career path. In general, if the element representing wealth features prominently in the birth data, the person will tend to become involved with money and finance—as in the case of Mr. Li. On the other hand, if the prominent element is not wealth, but power and status, the person is more likely to pursue a career associated with power. He may work in the civil service as an official or become an administrator in an organisation. In a more extreme case, he may become a politician.

Chairman Mao Tse-tung

The following set of Four Pillars of Destiny belongs to a major political figure—Chairman Mao Tse-tung, founder of the People's Republic of China:

The Pillars of Destiny of Chairman Mao (26/12/1893)

Hour	Day	Month	Year
甲 Wood	丁 Fire	甲 Wood	癸 Water
辰 Earth	酉 Metal	子 Water	巳 Fire

From his four pillars, we can see that he is a fire person born in the cold winter season when water is most prosperous. As the water element conquers fire, water symbolises power and status to a fire person. The water in Chairman Mao's pillars of destiny is not only in season, it also prominently occupies the heavenly stem of the year pillar. On the other hand, the element symbolising wealth—metal—occupies only one position in the earthly branches. It is obvious that power played a more important role than wealth in Chairman Mao's life and he was destined to become a politician.

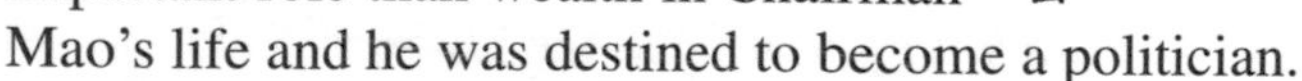

Rock Star David Bowie

Readers can easily appreciate the difference by observing the following set of pillars of destiny which bears some similarity to that of Chairman Mao Tse-tung.

The Pillars of Destiny of David Bowie (8/1/1947)

Hour	Day	Month	Year
甲	丁	辛	丙
Wood	Fire	Metal	Fire
辰	亥	丑	戌
Earth	Water	Earth	Earth

This person is also a fire person born under the same hour pillar as Chairman Mao. However, the most prominent element in his set of four pillars is earth, not water. The cycle of birth tells us that earth is given birth to by the fire element. So earth, to a fire person, symbolises aspirations and intelligence. A person with such a strong element of aspirations possesses a drive to express and present himself to the world. The elements symbolising the other aspects, such as power (water) and wealth (metal), are relatively weak. This person is neither a politician nor a businessman. He is the great performer and rock star—Mr. David Bowie.

These examples show the destiny of three famous men, each having great success and achievements in business, politics and entertainment, respectively. Their career potential are clearly reflected in their birth data translated into the Four Pillars of Destiny. In the same way, we can look up our birth date and time from a Chinese calendar and determine the prominent elements appearing in our own sets of Four Pillars of Destiny. If the element symbolising wealth is very strong, you are likely to be the business type. The next chapter will provide you with more guidelines to ascertain your potential in the business field.

Wealth In Your Destiny

I have shown readers how we can ascertain a person's business potential by examining his set of Four Pillars of Destiny. Often, as indicated by the examples in the previous chapter, the strong presence of the element representing wealth will reveal business potential. However, this is only a generalised statement and more details need to be examined carefully before we can be assured of our business ability.

In this chapter we will examine the element of wealth in more detail. The philosophy of the Four Pillars of Destiny is one of balance and harmony. If the element of wealth is excessively strong in a set of pillars of destiny, automatically, the element representing the self will be relatively weak. In such a case, the wealth element will be out of control and wealth beyond a person's control is not beneficial at all. This can be interpreted as either one of the following situations.

Firstly, the element of wealth is defined as the element conquered by the self. If we examine the cycle of birth and cycle of destruction more carefully, we can see that it is, at the same time, the element that gives birth to the element that conquers the self. If the self is wood, wealth is symbolised by earth. According to the cycle of birth, earth gives birth to metal, and according to the cycle of destruction, metal destroys wood—the self. Therefore, we can conclude that excessive wealth also creates a threat to the self, as wealth generates the element which destroys the self.

Thus, if you find too strong a wealth element in your destiny, you cannot immediately conclude that you can be a successful businessman. It is necessary to assess if the element on the heavenly stem of the day pillar (the self) is strong enough to control the wealth and to resist the element conquering the self. If the self is too weak, the plentiful wealth element will only generate more pressure and hardship, as symbolised by the element conquering the self. There is a well-known saying in the philosophy of the Four Pillars of Destiny—"Too much wealth will damage the health". People of weak self but very strong wealth and power elements may not automatically become successful businessman, but can be overwhelmed by financial problems.

There is another type of destiny which possesses much wealth, but not a very strong power element. This destiny is often found in people whose career is closely linked to money but who do not have the capacity to possess it. For example, a bank teller may spend much of his time counting money but the wealth does not belong to him and is totally beyond his control.

So do not be overjoyed if you find plenty of wealth elements in your destiny. You need to see further and evaluate if you are capable of controlling the wealth element. Similarly, do not be disappointed if you find many wealth elements but a weak self in your destiny. There are still opportunities to become a business tycoon. Mr. Li Ka-shing is a typical example, a very weak wood person surrounded by wealth elements, who managed to control his wealth to become a property tycoon.

The Role Of Luck Pillars

To help readers understand the mechanism of the Four Pillars of Destiny, I will now introduce another step in evaluating destiny—the listing of the luck pillars. From the birth data, we have obtained the Four Pillars of Destiny which are the birth year, month, day and hour of a person. This set of four pillars represents the components of the destiny of a person. However, it only shows us the inborn qualities, character, potential and environment of a person. When life begins, the person will receive influences from the universe in the form of the five elements, which will prevail all through his life path and interact with his original set of Four Pillars of Destiny to cause ups and downs in life.

These elemental influences are symbolised by a series of Chinese characters called the "Luck Pillars". These luck pillars can be derived from the month pillar of a set of Four Pillars of Destiny. Each luck pillar will show a period of ten years when the person will come under the influence of the two elements shown in each luck pillar. To be a fortunate person with great success in life, a person not only needs a set of good pillars of destiny, but also good luck pillars to support his pillars of destiny. We can compare the Four Pillars of Destiny to a car, and the series of luck pillars to a road. Even if the car is a Mercedes Benz, it still requires a good road to complete a good journey through life. If the road is bad and full of obstacles, even if the car is excellent, the journey will not be comfortable.

Thus, when evaluating the success of a person by examining his Four Pillars of Destiny, it is also necessary to see if his luck pillars are full of favourable elements and will give him the necessary support. A person born with a very good set of Four Pillars of Destiny may not necessarily be successful if he encounters very bad luck pillars. If such bad luck pillars occur early in life, it may even terminate the passage and the person may die young. In many cases, it is not just the Four Pillars of Destiny, but also the favourable luck pillars that contribute to success in life. (Appendix 3 shows the method of deriving the Luck Pillars from a set of Four Pillars of Destiny.)

How Li Ka-shing's Luck Pillars Helped Him

With this in mind, let us now examine the pillars of destiny of Mr. Li Kashing again, in conjunction with his luck pillars.

The Pillars of Destiny and Luck Pillars of Li Ka-shing

Hour	Day	Month	Year
?	甲 Wood	戊 Earth	戊 Earth
?	申 Metal	午 Fire	辰 Earth

68	58	48	38	28	18	8
乙 Wood	甲 Wood	癸 Water	壬 Water	辛 Metal	庚 Metal	己 Earth
丑 Earth	子 Water	亥 Water	戌 Earth	酉 Metal	申 Metal	未 Earth

Mr. Li is a man of wood born in the summer in a month of fire. Fire is most prosperous in summer and the strong fire exhausts Mr. Li's wood. In his known three pillars, year, month and day we cannot find any water to support and nourish the wood. Hence, the wood is very weak and he needs the support of water to survive. Water, in turn, needs the support of metal. It is easy therefore to see that Mr. Li's favourable elements are water and metal. On the other hand, fire and earth will consume and exhaust wood energy and are unfavourable elements.

The known pillars of destiny of Mr. Li Ka-shing show imbalance and disharmony with his wood being too weak while the unfavourable earth element is overly strong. But we cannot judge a person's potential from just his pillars of destiny. We must also observe his luck pillars to see if the weakness in his destiny can be compensated and cured by favourable elements in the luck pillars. In the case of Mr. Li, we can see that his early luck pillars at childhood before the age of 18 was the unfavourable earth element. This accurately reflects his poor background during childhood.

However, his fortune improved after the age of 18 as he entered the more favourable luck pillar of metal. It was about this time that he became the owner of a small plastic factory. But, metal, although a favourable element, is not as good as water which directly provides nourishment to wood. Good water influence eventually arrived at the age of 48 when he entered a very favourable luck pillar of strong water, and this favourable water influence continued into the next luck pillar and will last until the age of 68. This luck pillar represents the years from around 1976 to the present date. This is indeed the period when Mr. Li built up his vast property empire in Hong Kong and overseas and gained enormous wealth, earning the nickname "Mr. Superman".

This example shows clearly that we not only have to examine the status of the Four Pillars of Destiny first and evaluate the strengths and weaknesses of the five elements. We must also examine how the set of pillars of destiny will be affected by luck pillars during the person's passage through life. If the luck pillars are mostly favourable and supportive of the destiny, we can anticipate great potential of success. Otherwise, a well balanced set of pillars of destiny will bring little achievement if the luck pillars are not favourable. One general observation of the destiny of many successful people is that they are usually born with an imbalanced destiny with the self being excessively weak or strong. However, these people encounter very favourable elements in their luck pillars which offer panacea to their weak destiny and they are able to achieve great success. This is like a sick person who suddenly finds the right medicine to cure his disease.

By examining carefully the configuration of the wealth elements in relation to the self in our destiny, we can formulate a view about our potential to become a businessman and acquire wealth. Then we have to look at our luck pillars to confirm if the opportunities to achieve success are present. If they are, we can also check when the best timing is. Returning to Mr. Li's example, as it is obvious that the best influence of water will arrive at the age of around 48, a person with such insight into his destiny can devote his time before age 48 to educating and preparing himself for the arrival of the best luck pillar and the best year to make bold investments. His chances of success is almost assured by the favourable influence under the luck pillar.

When Is The Best Time To Invest?

As we have seen, each person has to pass through a series of luck pillars in his passage of life. These luck pillars represent elements which will exert influence on our destiny. If the luck pillar is favourable and supportive of the balance and harmony in our set of Four Pillars of Destiny, we are in a phase of good fortune and business ventures undertaken during this time will be favourable and smooth. On the other hand, if we transit into a luck pillar containing unfavourable elements which exaggerate the imbalance or disharmony in our destiny, we will find life full of obstacles and our business decisions will tend to be faulty.

Indeed, people in the business field will fully agree with me that no matter how intelligently one makes decisions in business, there is always the factor of luck which is totally beyond human control. Sudden events such as natural disasters, accidents, political changes, weather, acts of God, *force majeur*, civil disturbances and war are factors which can turn a very profitable venture into a disaster. The key to avoiding such mishaps is to avoid bad luck when entering business ventures. And to avoid bad luck, the only means is to thoroughly understand our own destiny and carefully choose the good cycles in life to take business risks.

First Determine Your Luck Pillar

In the previous examples, I have pointed out that each person is governed by a series of luck pillars which lasts for ten years. Before taking substantial business risks, the first step is to determine whether we are in a good luck pillar. A good luck pillar refers to one which contains favourable elements. Returning to the example of Mr. Li Ka-shing, his good luck pillar from the age of 48 to 58 is represented by water, his favourite element. If a person discovers himself in such a good luck pillar, he will be in the best position to speculate and invest. His investments are more likely to result in good profit. In other words, almost everything he touches will turn into gold.

However, in real life, not everyone can have a good luck pillar of pure favourable elements like Mr. Li Ka-shing. In many cases we will find we are into a luck pillar which is a combination of good and bad. For example, a weak fire person in need of wood support may encounter a luck pillar which is wood and earth with wood in the heavenly stem and earth in the earthly branches. In such case, he has to be more careful. As a general rule, the heavenly stem will prevail in the first five years and the earthly branches will prevail in the next five years. This weak fire person should exploit his chances in the first five years and refrain from risky ventures in the second half of the luck pillar—the next five years.

In practice, a luck pillar of ten years is a long time and there are still ups and downs from year to year. A person who is into a good ten-year luck pillar may observe that within the ten years, some years are better than others. Besides examining the influence of the luck pillar, we also need to carefully examine the impact of the year, or even the day, the month, or the hour.

As mentioned at the beginning of this book, the Chinese calendar is a calendar expressing time in terms of the five basic elements. This is the foundation on which the Chinese establish the link between human fortune and destiny with the universe. Human destiny, as represented by the bundle of elements prevailing at the time of our birth, is also subject to elemental influences from the universe. Such elemental influence changes from year to year, day to day, and hour to hour, and the pattern of change is clearly expressed by the heavenly stems and earthly branches shown on the Chinese Hsia calendar.

In the Chinese calendar, each item of time, year, month, day and hour, is also expressed by the set of ten heavenly stems and twelve earthly branches which we use in the Four Pillars of Destiny. These heavenly stems and earthly branches symbolise the influence of the five basic elements. These elements exert favourable or unfavourable influence on human destiny continuously and it is through such continuous influence and interaction of the five elements that events and activities occur in this universe.

By such a system of elemental patterns and interrelationships, we can, in theory, determine the outcome of events with accuracy down to the hour. Of course, to describe small events from a bundle of elements is very technical. But it is still possible. It is beyond the scope of this book to break down our analysis into such minor details. However, by applying such a system, we can accurately forecast the most favourable moment to invest with a considerable degree of certainty.

Li Ka-shing's Perfect Timing

Returning to the familiar example of Mr. Li Ka-shing, we can see that he has made some very wise business decisions with perfect timing. Mr. Li successfully listed his property empire—Cheung Kong Property Holdings—in the Hong Kong Stock Market in the year 1972. At the time, he was 44 and in the favourable luck pillar of water and earth. And the year 1972 was a year of very strong water which is his favourable element. Subsequently, in the year 1979 and at the age of 51, when he was in the most favourable luck pillar of pure water influence, he again surprised the world by taking over the Hutchison Group, which become a very profitable arm of his Cheung Kong empire.

All businessmen realise the importance of right timing in doing business but they have no way to assure themselves that they have taken the right step at the right time. Just like speculators in the stock market. All speculators want to avoid buying when the market is still on a downward trend but it is impossible to know in advance whether the market has already bottomed out or will continue to fall. The Four Pillars of Destiny is able to offer an answer to such dilemma. The way to make such a decision to invest or not is to carefully examine one's pillars of destiny and ask the following questions:

- Am I in a favourable luck pillar?
- Am I in a favourable year and are the yearly elements supportive of my destiny?
- Is the immediate future, say the next six to 12 months, favourable?
- Are there any signs of strong competition for wealth? If there are, what is my competitor's strength compared to mine.

If all the answers are positive and favourable, it is very likely that the venture will be successful, at least in the short term.

At this juncture, I think it is necessary to explain the last question regarding competition in greater detail. If the element representing the self is wood, then the wood element also symbolises colleagues and friends, or people in similar position and status. If the self is weak, such colleagues can be helpful as they can be friends coming to share the workload or pressure. On the other hand, if the self is strong, then such assistance is not necessary and will only increase the excessive strength of the self, causing further imbalance in the destiny. Under such circumstances, these are not friends but foes. They are often symbols of strong competition as there is danger of these competitors snatching away wealth from the self. If such competitors appear in a certain year, it is necessary to compare the element of the year against the self element to see which is stronger. If the element appearing in the year is comparatively stronger, it is likely that one will lose in the competition and it is inadvisable to take substantial business risks in such a year.

George Bush versus Bill Clinton

The best example to illustrate such a situation is the competition between the then incumbent President Bush and the Democrat candidate, the present President Clinton, in the 1992 U.S. Presidential election. Let us examine President Bush's pillars of destiny.

The Pillars of Destiny and Luck Pillars of President Bush

Hour	Day	Month	Year
?	壬 Water	庚 Metal	甲 Wood
?	戌 Earth	午 Fire	子 Water

68	58	48	38	28	18
丁 Fire	丙 Fire	乙 Wood	甲 Wood	癸 Water	壬 Water
丑 Earth	子 Water	亥 Water	戌 Earth	酉 Metal	申 Metal

The pillars show that President Bush is a water person born in the summer when fire is most prosperous. He is a weak water person and requires the support of metal and water. The Presidential election was held in 1992—

a year of strong water and metal. In theory it is a favourable year for President Bush and he should have good chance of winning the election.

But if President Bush had asked himself the four questions listed earlier in this chapter at the beginning of 1992, his answers would have been as follows:

- The Luck pillar effect. At the age of 68, he is moving from the favourable luck pillar of water into the comparatively less favourable luck pillar of fire. However, the favourable water influence remains strong as 1992 is a year of strong water and metal.
- The year effect. As President Bush's favourable elements are metal and water, 1992, being a year of strong water and metal elements, is certainly a good year for him in general.
- The 12 months ahead. The year following 1992–93 is another year of metal and water, which is still favourable to President Bush.
- The competition effect. The year 1992 is very strong water overlying metal. As President Bush is also a water person, this means a strong man of comparable status is emerging to compete against him for the Presidency. Therefore it is necessary to determine who is stronger. We see that President Bush is a water person sitting on earth which is a destructive element to water. He is a weak water person. On the other hand, his competitor appearing in 1992 is symbolised by a water person sitting on metal; water gaining support from metal is obviously stronger.

So, for questions one to three, President Bush is able to answer favourably but the answer to question four upsets everything. Despite 1992 being a good year with good fortune, President Bush was unable to win because his competitor was stronger.

The same logic can easily be applied to our business ventures. If we see an element similar to the self appearing in the year or in the critical month of the venture, it is important to pause to evaluate if this symbolises a very strong competitor appearing—a competitor who may snatch away our benefits from the business venture. Such caution, as illustrated in the example of President Bush, is essential in choosing the right time to enter a business venture.

Choosing The Right Business

With a clearer concept of wealth in our destiny, we can now determine whether we possess the potential to start our own business (in the case where our wealth element is prominent and under control), or if it is better to remain in a secure job as an employee in an organisation (in the case where the power element is more prominent than the wealth, or where the self is too weak to control wealth). There are many career channels we can choose according to the potential reflected in our destiny. Supposing we are convinced that we are the business type and see opportunity in our luck pillars to acquire more wealth. Then the next question to ask is: which is the most appropriate business field to invest our money in?

The philosophy of the Four Pillars of Destiny states that everything in the universe is composed of the five basic elements. Thus, we can assign even careers and business fields to an element. Some industries are very obviously associated with an element. For example, the property business is clearly related to the earth element, the shipping business is symbolised by metal and water elements, and the fashion, textile and paper industries, which use materials made from plants, are represented by the wood element.

For easy reference, the following table shows the elemental symbols for some common industries and businesses:

Metal — gold, steelwork, metalwork, cars, jewellery
Wood — paper, textile, fashion, furniture
Water — shipping, dyeing, beverages

Fire — energy, cooking, electricity, electronics
Earth — property, construction, mining, chemicals

These are some obvious examples. However, modern society is complex and there are many service industries whose nature cannot be easily classified into an element. Some of these unique business fields require special judgement before they can be related to an element. For instance, careers which require much talking, can, in fact, be classified under the metal category. The reason is that the metal element is also a symbol of the mouth.

From my previous experience, the fire element is related to finance and the stock market. I have observed the destinies of some financial people and stockbrokers whose destiny is often closely related to the fire element. Wall Street's stock market fluctuations also show a close correlation to the influence of the fire element. (A more detailed analysis of the stock market performance will be presented in a later chapter of this book).

The wood element is a symbol of fibre and hair as I have observed a prominent wood element in the destinies of hairstylists.

These examples indicate how we can classify various modern industries into five basic elements. Equipped with such knowledge, we can then decide which field is most suitable for a business venture. Again, the Four Pillars of Destiny provides us with a guide to making the right choice.

As discussed in the previous chapters, after listing our Four Pillars of Destiny, we have to establish which are our favourable elements that will bring harmony and balance to the set of four pillars. In theory, it is best for us to enter the field represented by the most favourable element to our destiny. In the case of a weak fire person, his favourable element is wood, as wood will provide support and nourishment to the weak fire. The most favourable industry for this fire person is a wood-related industry, such as furniture, paper or textile. On the other hand, he should avoid getting into shipping, as shipping is symbolised by water and the water element will destroy the weak fire. This is a generalised theory, under the assumption that we have plenty of free choices, and that freewill prevails over destiny.

Whether freewill can control our destiny is a philosophical question and can generate much debate. It is beyond the scope of this chapter to delve deeper into this subject. Interested readers can find more discussion on the topic at the end of the book. However, from my personal experience with the study of destiny, it appears rather idealistic to say a person can enter an industry which is most favourable to his destiny. In real life, this is often not the case. Instead, people often enter a field, not represented by his favourable elements, but represented by the most prominent and strongest elements in his destiny.

What Drives Li Ka-shing

Let us again use property tycoon Mr. Li Ka-shing's pillars of destiny for illustration. As explained in the previous chapter, Mr. Li is a weak wood person and his favourable elements should be water and metal. However, instead of making a name for himself in the shipping business, Mr. Li Ka-shing is well known for his success in property which falls into the category of earth. But earth is his unfavourable element. This seems to contradict the theory that one should pursue a career which is represented by one's most favourable element.

It is easy to see that Mr. Li pursued a career related to the earth element because the earth element is prominent and dominates his Four Pillars of Destiny. Hence there is already a driving force in his destiny leading him there. While earth is not his favourable element, once he gained water support from his luck pillars at the age of 48, his wood self became strong enough to keep the unfavourable earth element under control and turned it into his enormous property-generated wealth.

Property Tycoon Alan Bond

At this point, it will be interesting for us to examine the pillars of destiny of another famous property tycoon—Mr. Alan Bond of Australia.

The Pillars of Destiny of Alan Bond (22/4/1938)

Hour	Day	Month	Year
?	甲 Wood	丙 Fire	戊 Earth
?	申 Metal	辰 Earth	寅 Wood

From his set of pillars of destiny, we can observe a close similarity to Mr. Li Kashing. Both Mr. Bond and Mr. Li are wood persons and both sets of destiny possess dominating earth elements—symbolising their wealth. It is little wonder then that both men made their fortunes from property.

Mr. Supertanker—Sir Y.K. Pao

For contrast, let us examine the destiny of another famous Hong Kong tycoon, the "King of the Sea" or "Mr. Supertanker", Sir Y.K. Pao who acquired enormous wealth from his fleet of supertankers in the 60s and early 70s. The following is his set of pillars of destiny.

The Pillars of Destiny of Sir Y.K. Pao (10/11/1918)

Hour	Day	Month	Year
?	辛 Metal	癸 Water	戊 Earth
?	酉 Metal	亥 Water	午 Earth

69	59	49	39	29	19	9
庚 Metal	己 Earth	戊 Earth	丁 Fire	丙 Fire	乙 Wood	甲 Wood
午 Fire	巳 Fire	辰 Earth	卯 Wood	寅 Wood	丑 Earth	子 Water

Sir Y.K. Pao is a metal person born in the winter season when the water element is most prosperous. As water exhausts metal, Sir Y.K. can be considered a weak metal person, relying on the earth element to provide nourishment and support. The earth elements, in turn, need the warmth of fire, as fire gives birth to earth. Thus, fire and earth are both favourable elements to Sir Y.K. Water, however, is unfavourable as it weakens his metal strength.

Yet, instead of plunging into the property business, as his favourable earth element suggests, Sir Y.K. achieved great success in shipping, which falls

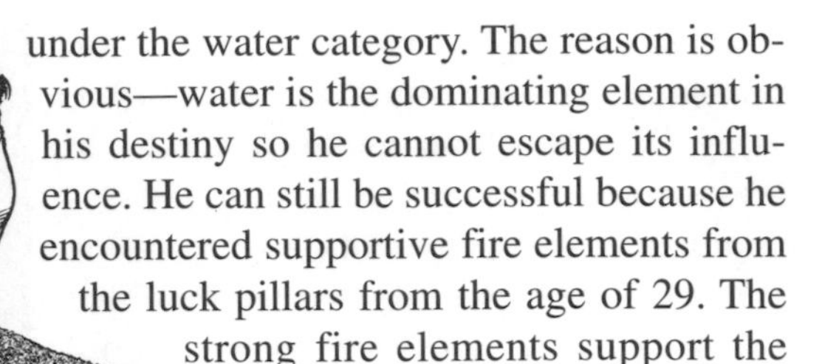

under the water category. The reason is obvious—water is the dominating element in his destiny so he cannot escape its influence. He can still be successful because he encountered supportive fire elements from the luck pillars from the age of 29. The strong fire elements support the earth in his destiny which in turn provides support to the metal self.

The metal has become strong enough to withstand the flooding water. This is the reason behind his success in a water business—shipping. Interestingly, Sir Y.K. gradually diversified into the property business and became a major property owner in the prosperous Tsim Sha Tsui area in Kowloon. This change is also reflected in his destiny. At the age of 49, Sir Y.K. reached a luck pillar which is very strong earth. The strong earth element suppressed the water and became a dominating element in the configuration. This change of power from water to earth caused Sir Y.K.'s business focus to change from shipping to property.

These examples cast much light on the mystery of how we are led into a certain career or field. To summarise, it appears that the strongest or dominating element in our destiny often provides the driving force to lead us into a career associated with such an element, regardless of whether the element is favourable or not. Once we have been driven into such a career, whether we can achieve success or not is determined by our ability to control and manipulate the element. If the luck pillars can provide enough support to enhance the strength of the self, so that the self is capable of keeping the unfavourable element under control, the person will often achieve great success in the field even if it is not his favourable element.

With this knowledge, we can now establish some guidelines in selecting our career. The first step is to look for the most favourable element in our destiny. If this element is strong and dominating, we can easily enter the industry represented by the element and achieve great success. On the other hand, if the favourable element is weak and is not enhanced significantly by our luck pillars, it will be difficult for us to enter such a career. In this case, the person is likely to be driven, willingly or with reluctance, into a career that is symbolised by the dominating but unfavourable element in his destiny. But this does not mean he is bound to fail. As we have seen from the enlightening examples of Mr. Li Ka-shing and Sir Y.K. Pao, great success is still a possibility as long as the luck pillar can enhance the strength of the self to keep the unfavourable element under control.

How To Select The Right Partner

A problem a businessman often encounters is whether to enter a partnership with another person, or whether to team up with another person in a business venture. There are many questions to ask before we can make such a decision. Firstly, we need to judge if the venture is economically viable or profitable. Then we must also determine if the partner in the venture is compatible and if there will be harmony in the cooperation. Very often a profitable joint venture is ruined by conflicting characters among the partners. After all, one cannot expect a business venture to proceed smoothly if the key partners are always quarrelling and find it difficult to reach a mutual agreement on policy. In a previous chapter, I have already discussed the problem of the right timing to take up a profitable venture. In this chapter, let us shift our focus from profitability to human harmony in a business venture. We will see how we can employ Chinese metaphysics to select the best partner for running a business smoothly.

The Four Pillars of Destiny offer several ways to judge compatibility in human relationships. Selecting a partner, in some ways, is like selecting a wife or husband as harmony and compatibility in character is one basic requirement. In the method of the Four Pillars of Destiny, the way to achieve harmony is to enhance the elements which will bring about balance to a person's set of four pillars. In other words, one fundamental rule for a matching partnership is that both partners' pillars of destiny possess plenty of elements favourable to the other. If one person is a weak fire requiring more wood for support and nourishment, he will find another person very compatible if this other person's pillars of destiny contain plenty of wood and fire. This is because the man with plenty of wood will serve and supplement the needs of the man with very weak fire. If the man of weak fire possesses plenty of earth in his destiny, he will also be compatible with the man with strong wood as he needs earth to exhaust the excessive wood energy. This kind of partnership is considered mutually beneficial and will be harmonious at least in the aspect of human relationships.

Japan's Royal Couple—Naruhito And Owada

Let us examine the following example of a couple considered compatible with each other. This famous pair of pillars of destiny belongs to Crown Prince Naruhito and Princess Owada of Japan.

The Pillars of Destiny of Crown Prince Naruhito (23/2/1960)

	Hour	Day	Month	Year	
	?	辛 Metal	戊 Earth	庚 Metal	
	?	巳 Fire	寅 Wood	子 Water	
54	44	34	24	14	4
甲 Wood	癸 Water	壬 Water	辛 Metal	庚 Metal	己 Earth
申 Metal	未 Earth	午 Fire	巳 Fire	辰 Earth	卯 Wood

The Pillars of Destiny of Princess Owada (9/12/1963)

	Hour	Day	Month	Year
	?	丙 Fire	甲 Wood	癸 Water
	?	戊 Earth	子 Water	卯 Wood
50	40	30	20	10
己 Earth	戊 Earth	丁 Fire	丙 Fire	乙 Wood
巳 Fire	辰 Earth	卯 Wood	寅 Wood	丑 Earth

These pillars of destiny show that the Crown Prince is a metal person born in February—a season of wood—when the metal is not prosperous. He is, therefore, a weak metal person and needs the support of earth, which in turn needs support from fire. His compatible partner should possess substantial earth and fire elements in her destiny to meet his needs.

Let us examine the pillars of destiny of Princess Owada. She is fire lady born in the cold winter when water is most prosperous. Water is the destroyer of fire. So she is a weak fire lady and needs the support of wood. She should, therefore, look for a husband or compatible partner who possesses sufficient wood in his destiny. Armed with such knowledge, let us cross-examine both the Crown Prince and the Princess's destinies again to see if they can meet each other's criteria as a compatible couple.

The Princess needs the support of wood; this she can sufficiently find in the Crown Prince's month pillar as the Prince was born in February—a season of very strong wood. On the other hand, the Crown Prince is looking for the support of the fire and earth elements in his partner's destiny. Looking at the Princess's four pillars, we can see her day pillar is fire on earth which meets the requirement. Although the fire is not strong, at the age of 30 in 1993, she was under the influence of strong wood and fire from her prevailing luck pillar. Therefore, they are a compatible couple and can meet each other's elemental needs.

This example illustrates how we can select a compatible partner to ensure that the human relationship in the joint venture is harmonious. However, human harmony is seldom the main objective in a business venture. The focus is more on profitability. Therefore it is essential to examine the aspect of wealth in the prospective partner's destiny before making a decision to team up with him.

In the previous chapters, we have already emphasized the importance of timing in taking business risks. After applying the test of business potential on ourselves, we can apply the same test on a prospective partner. The simple logic is that a partner in good fortune is an indication that the business venture will be profitable, as his good fortune may help to bring benefit and profit to the joint venture. On the other hand, a partner in bad luck may bring damage and obstacles to the business venture. It is certainly desirable to find a partner whose pillars of destiny reflect that he is in the best of luck or that he is well poised to gain substantial wealth. With such a strong partner, you may be able to share his good fortune by teaming up with him.

Mr. Universe—Arnold Schwarzenegger

To illustrate this point, let us look at the Four Pillars of Destiny of Hollywood superstar Mr. Arnold Schwarzenegger.

The Pillars of Destiny of Arnold Schwarzenegger (30/7/1947)

Hour	Day	Month	Year
戊 Earth	庚 Metal	丁 Fire	丁 Fire
寅 Wood	戌 Earth	未 Earth	亥 Water

57	47	37	27	17	7
辛 Metal	壬 Water	癸 Water	甲 Wood	乙 Wood	丙 Fire
丑 Earth	寅 Wood	卯 Wood	辰 Earth	巳 Fire	午 Fire

As the pillars show, Mr. Schwarzenegger is a metal person born in a month of earth. There are plenty of earth elements in the destiny to provide nourishment to the metal. Hence the metal is strong. It is interesting to note that earth also symbolises flesh and muscle in the human body and the strong earth element obviously matches well with Mr. Schwarzenegger's powerful physique and his many Mr. Universe titles. However, as we are discussing business, the focus is on Mr. Schwarzenegger's money making potential. In this respect, we can see that Mr. Schwarzenegger, being a strong metal person, is in good position to control and manipulate wealth once he encounters it in his destiny or in his luck pillars. As discussed previously, wealth is defined as the element conquered by the self. Mr. Schwarzenegger is a metal man. His wealth is represented by the wood element. As wood relies on water to grow, the water element symbolises the money making potential or intelligence in the person.

After the age of 37, Mr. Schwarzenegger entered a period with strong water and wood influences which will dominate two consecutive luck pillars up to the age of 57. These strong water and wood elements all symbolise money and the strongest wood is expected to appear in the luck pillar for the ten year period between the age 47 to 57. Indeed, it was at the age of 37 that Mr. Schwarzenegger released his hit movie *Conan the Barbarian* in 1982. Thereafter he became one of the most popular action heroes on movie screens throughout the world and his earnings have reached astronomical figures in recent years. If you were fortunate enough to have taken up a joint venture business with Mr. Schwarzenegger, the business would almost certainly have been profitable and successful.

This is an example of how one can assess the impact of a potential partner in a business venture. As the main objective is profitability, we cannot afford to team up with a partner who is in bad luck and is not in a position to generate profit. Besides concern about a harmonious relationship with a partner, it is even more vital to evaluate his destiny to see if he is in good business fortune. If the business partner satisfies both criteria, then the success of the joint venture business is almost assured.

Guide To Hiring And Managing Employees

Today, many large corporations use psychological or aptitude tests to hire staff. The purpose of these tests is to ensure that the staff they employ are suitable for the positions. Very few professionals in personnel management, however, realise that this goal of placing the right person in the right job can be achieved more effectively through metaphysical means. In this chapter, I will demonstrate how we can employ the technique of the Four Pillars of Destiny in personnel management and staff appointment.

We have seen how we can select a beneficial partner when taking up a joint venture. The qualities we look for in a partner are favourable and complementary elements to meet our needs, as well as good fortune to enhance profitability. Using the same logic, we can employ the technique in staff selection. However, we can now shift our focus slightly to emphasize the nature of the work the prospective employee is supposed to carry out.

Firstly, we should look at the destiny of the prospective employee to ensure his compatibility with the prospective boss. This is necessary to maintain a harmonious relationship in the office, and to avoid character conflict which may reduce work efficiency. We have already thoroughly discussed this aspect in the last chapter on selecting a compatible partner.

Secondly, I would suggest that an employer look for reasonably good luck in a prospective employee to ensure good performance and job satisfaction. It is logical to expect a happy and healthy employee to perform better than one who is always in grave trouble and often encounters obstacles. Often, a fortunate salesman with high scores will bring more benefit and profit to the boss and to the company.

Besides these factors, the Four Pillars of Destiny can also offer considerable insight into the potential of the prospective employee in a certain career. This can be obtained from the dominating element in the Four Pillars of Destiny.

In the previous chapters, we have discussed how we should recognise our potential to determine which career and direction is most suitable. By the same token, we can employ the same technique in selecting the right employee to fill a position. Different persons are born with different career potential and it is a waste of effort and time to train up someone only to discover later that his interest is not in the field at all.

Through the philosophy of the Four Pillars of Destiny, we can categorise career potential into four major types. Namely, the power type, the money type, the creative type and the academic type. In this chapter we will analyse these four areas one by one.

The Power Type

The power type refers to people whose destiny is dominated by the power element, which is defined as the element conquering the self. If the self is fire, and the person is born in winter with water dominating, then he is the power type. The reason is that water destroys fire, so the prominent water element is a symbol of power and status to a fire person.

An extreme example is the pillars of destiny of Chairman Mao of China. A fire person born in winter, with power and status most prominent in his destiny, he became one of the greatest political figures of the twentieth century.

A person with a very prominent power element, like Chairman Mao and many other politicians and powerful leaders, tends to associate himself with politics and power play. However, a person with a prominent power element which is not as strong as that of Chairman Mao may not turn to politics, but instead become a very capable administrator or manager in a big organisation. If the position is administrative in nature, it is wiser to select an employee with stronger power elements. Such persons are often disciplined, authoritative and firm with leadership and management potential.

The Money Type

The money type are those with a prominent money or wealth element in their destiny. The money element is defined as the element that the self conquers. For example, to a wood person, earth is his wealth element. In previous chapters, we have already seen many examples of the money type. We can again refer to the extreme cases of Mr. Li Ka-shing and Mr. Alan Bond who are both wood persons with the prominent wealth element of earth in their destiny.

As we have seen, people with a strong money element in their destiny and who encounter strong fortune in their luck pillar to control the money may become as rich as Mr. Li. However, in most cases of people with a strong money element in their destiny, the self is too weak to keep the money under control. If they do not encounter very good luck pillars to enable them to control the wealth, these people will not become tycoons like Mr. Li. But they can still perform credibly as financial controllers, accountants or bank clerks in an organisation, depending on how well their luck pillars support them in their passage through life. The following is another example of a person with a prominent money element in his destiny:

The Pillars of Destiny of Sir Pier Jacobs (27/5/1933)

Hour	Day	Month	Year
?	癸 Water	丁 Fire	癸 Water
?	巳 Fire	巳 Fire	酉 Metal

This set of pillars belongs to the former Financial Secretary of the Hong Kong government—Sir Pier Jacobs. He is a man of water born in the summer season when fire is the most prosperous element. In his three known pillars, fire is plentiful and prominent. It is obvious that a person with such a strong wealth element is destined to handle considerable sums of money in his career.

The Creative Type

We have so far introduced the administrative type and the money type. However, on many occasions, an employer may look for a designer or a salesman for jobs of a more creative or outgoing nature. For such jobs, you may want to employ a creative type. The creative element in our destiny is defined as the element that is given birth by the self. If the self is the fire element, fire gives birth to earth. Earth is then considered the creative element to a fire person. People with plenty of creative elements usually present themselves with intelligence and eloquence, and dress well. This type of character potential is suitable for jobs which demand a more outgoing and creative type of personality. Persons who possess a very prominent creative element may even become famous movie stars, singers or performers. The following is an example of the four pillars of a great singer and performer:

The Pillars of Destiny of David Bowie (8/1/1947)

Hour	Day	Month	Year
甲 Wood	丁 Fire	辛 Metal	丙 Fire
辰 Earth	亥 Water	丑 Earth	戌 Earth

This is the destiny of the British rock and roll star Mr. David Bowie who is renowned for his considerable talent in singing, song composition as well as his performances on stage and in movies. His destiny shows he is a fire person with very prominent and plentiful earth elements. As fire gives birth to earth, earth is his creative element. Mr. David Bowie is an outstanding example of how a person with a creative element in his destiny can achieve great success in fields requiring creativity.

The example of Mr. David Bowie is an extreme case. In ordinary creative jobs, we do not require too many creative elements. In fact, it is necessary to avoid having too strong a creative element. The reason is that creative elements are generated from the self. An excessive creative element will exhaust the self and make the self element too weak. Therefore it is necessary to have some control over excessive creative elements in a set of pillars of destiny. To be capable of creating, one must possess sufficient resources. The element we normally require to balance the creative element is called the resources element. This is defined as the element that gives birth to the self.

As Mr. David Bowie is a fire person, his resource element is wood, as wood gives birth to fire. Without the support of wood, he is too weak to generate the earth. So it is necessary to look for sufficient resource element after finding plenty of creative element in a set of destiny. The normal phenomenon is that people with an excessive creative element but insufficient resource element will be talkative but without depth and substance in their speech. These are like empty bottles making the most noise. On the other hand, people with some creative element who also possess sufficient resource element are often skilful professionals.

The Academic Type

Finally there is yet another type of person whose dominating elements are not money, power or creativity but the resource element. These people often gravitate towards research and academic world and are best suited for jobs requiring planning and research. Examples would be economists, scientists or training officers in a large corporation. To demonstrate, let us look at the pillars of destiny of a prominent scientist—Mr. Albert Einstein.

The Pillars of Destiny of Albert Einstein (1879)

Hour	Day	Month	Year
癸 Water	丙 Fire	丁 Fire	己 Earth
巳 Fire	申 Metal	卯 Wood	卯 Wood

Mr. Einstein is a fire person born in the spring when wood is most prosperous. To a fire person, wood is the mother of fire and is thus his resource element. The strong wood element in Mr. Einstein's destiny enabled him to achieve great success in scientific research.

We have now seen the four major types of elements which can have a profound influence on a person's career potential. They can provide guidelines for an employer to evaluate the aptitude of a prospective employee for any position.

In this chapter, we have discussed the selection of a prospective employee according to his aptitude. However, the real business world is far more complicated and there are other factors to consider besides personal aptitude. In a previous chapter I have already introduced the skill of classifying different industries under different elements. For example, fire is related to finance, energy and electricity while metal is related to jewellery and metalwork. This technique is useful to provide us some hint about how long an employee will stay in a certain industry. If, for example, you are a car dealer, an employee with plenty of metal elements in his destiny will stay in the industry longer than others, as the car is symbolised by the metal element.

Finally, I also recommend that you evaluate the fortune profile of a prospective employee, at least for the immediate future. It is logical to employ a worker with good prospects of promotion and success ahead of him. Therefore, when screening applicants, select those who are expected to encounter favourable years or luck pillars in the near future.

Forecasting Prosperity In The Stock Market

In the earlier chapters, I have demonstrated the fascinating technique of the Four Pillars of Destiny in helping to make important business decisions. However, the potential of this profound art of Chinese metaphysics is far from being thoroughly explored. Besides being effectively employed as a tool in forecasting human fortune, the Four Pillars of Destiny can be used to assess larger issues such the world economy, the ups and downs of the stock market, and even events like wars and upheavals that can have substantial impact on business ventures.

I have, in articles published in the *Hong Kong Standard* between 1988 and 1991, successfully predicted the emergence and outcome of important events such as the Gulf War, the resignation of Mrs. Margaret Thatcher and the fall of President Mikhail Gorbachev from power. In all these cases, the tool used to make such forecasts was nothing more than the Four Pillars of Destiny. The reason is simple—most world events are greatly influenced by certain individuals and the destinies of these individuals or world leaders can reveal the course of development of the events. For example, through the pillars of destiny of Saddam Hussein and President Bush, we can detect a major conflict and struggle between the metal and the wood element in the spring of 1991. These are signs of war and it enabled me to forecast the outbreak of the Gulf war.

By the same token, the demise of the power elements in the destiny of Mrs. Margaret Thatcher and President Gorbachev in the years between 1991 and 1992 again revealed their impending fall from power and authority.

Through the pillars of destiny of some key world leaders, it is possible to forecast their success or failure, which, in turn, will cast light on the course of the nations that they represent. For persons whose businesses are strongly linked to international trade and the global economy, some advance knowledge about political affairs or the economic trend is of paramount importance to their business decisions. This chapter is, therefore, devoted to the analysis of world trends through the application of Chinese metaphysical techniques.

I have given examples of how I employed the Four Pillars of Destiny to predict political events. We can also forecast economic performance using the same technique.

The economist considers macro economic behaviour as the collective behaviour of the micro individuals. As each individual possesses his own personal fortune as reflected by the Four Pillars of Destiny, it is possible to assess the trend of economic performance by observing the economic fortune of many individuals. An obvious example is immediately prior to the collapse of the global stock market in October 1987, when the author was able to observe signs of financial crisis in many clients' pillars of destiny.

Through analysing the destiny of people who are major investors or key players in the stock market, or whose wealth and wellbeing are closely related to the stock market, it is possible to see the trend of economic performance by observing the collective tendency of the fortunes of these people. After studying the pillars of destiny of many people who speculate in the stock market, I noticed some correlation between the fire element and the stock market's performance. The hypothesis is that a strong configuration of the fire element is often associated with economic boom and a bullish stock market. On the other hand, the weakening or demise of the fire element seems to have a strong correlation with a bearish market and a depressed economy.

Charting Wall Street's Stock Market Collapses

This correlation between the fire element and stock market performance can be illustrated by examining the timing of the stock market collapses in the history of Wall Street. Many stockbrokers have noticed that October is often a month of instability for the stock market and some major collapses have occur in or around October. The most prominent examples are the October 1929 and October 1987 collapses. This phenomenon can also be explained by the theory that stock market performance is closely related to the fire element. October is the autumn season symbolising the decline of the fire element after the passing of the summer season when fire is at its peak of prosperity.

However, we need to learn some niceties before we can formulate a useful metaphysical theory about the stock market performance. Despite autumn being the season when the stock market becomes vulnerable, a market collapse does not occur in October every year. To explain this, we need a deeper understanding of the system of the Chinese calendar.

To recap, the Chinese Hsia calendar describes each year in terms of two characters, each representing an element. These two characters are called the heavenly stems and earthly branches. One heavenly stem and one earthly branch pair up to form the name of a year. The significance of these stems and branches is that each one represents an element. So the name of a year, shown in the form of heavenly stems and earthly branches, in fact, tells us which elements are at play in a certain year.

For example, the year 1986 is named "丙寅", which is yang fire on the heavenly stem and yang wood on the earthly branch. According to our hypothesis that fire is related to the stock market, 1986, with the influence of strong wood enhancing the power of strong fire, was a year of global economic boom with many making money from investments in the stock market. Despite the above theory, we did not experience a stock market collapse in the autumn of 1986. The reason is that although autumn is the season when the fire element is weak, the power of fire remained strong as the subsequent year, 1987, is represented by the Chinese characters "丁卯", which is yin fire and yin wood. Thus, there was continuity in the fire influence from 1986 to 1987 with no demise of the fire element in the autumn of 1986. The stock market remained strong in the autumn and winter of 1986 with fire power prevailing.

Let us now look at the year 1987—a year of yin fire. The fire power is weaker than that of 1986. However, the fire element continues to support the stock market in the summer of 1987 and the performance remained strong until October, when the world experienced a collapse. Again we have to look beyond the year 1987 to explain what happened in the autumn of 1987. The year after 1987 is 1988, a year described in the Chinese calendar as earth on the heavenly stem and earth on the earthly branch (戊辰). As fire gives birth to earth, the earth element is detrimental to the fire power because it will exhaust fire energy. Without the continuity of the fire power into 1988, the fire power began declining in the autumn of 1987. It was this demise of the fire element in the autumn of 1987 that caused the global stock market collapse in October 1987.

The theory of linking the fire element to the global economic performance can also be tested in the years following 1987. The world economy recovered quickly in 1989 and 1990 and these two years were years of earth and fire, and metal and fire, respectively. However, entering the year of metal and earth in 1991 (辛未), the economic atmosphere in the U.S. and the West deteriorated considerably and the depression worsened in the strong metal and water years of 1992 (壬申) and 1993 (癸酉). According to the theory, signs of real recovery can only be expected with the return of wood and earth in the year 1994 (甲戌). However, the recovery will only be temporary as the power of wood in 1994 is not strong enough to support the fire element. Furthermore, we are still within the water cycle and the strongest water influence will come in 1996, a year of fire over water (丙子), when we can expect another setback in economic performance.

A Word Of Caution

This discussion provides readers with a crude guideline on the assessment of risk in the stock market if your business is closely related to finance and speculation. However, I have to caution that the technique of the Four Pillars of Destiny is only designed to analyse individual fortunes. The application of this technique on macro events like economic trends still have some fallacies. Firstly, the assumption that players in the stock market favour fire is based on empirical observations of past events. However, as time changes and the old players pass on, a different generation of players will emerge whose destiny could favour elements other than fire. Moreover, the mechanism of the stock market game is now changing. With the introduction of new instruments such as index trading, a booming stock market will not necessarily mean the majority will profit. Readers will need to bear in mind such pitfalls and adapt to the changing circumstances when applying the technique. The most reliable method is still to examine the money prospect in our own pillars of destiny before speculating.

As discussed earlier, we can assign the five basic elements to different industries. I therefore recommend that readers make a careful study of their particular industry and attempt to identify some correlation of their industry with an element. You can then use it as a tool to forecast the prosperity of your own special industry.

At this juncture, I have to point out that the strong presence of an element representing an industry often does not bring prosperity to the industry. To the contrary, it often causes a down cycle. For example, the price of gold does not rise, but often plummets in a year when the metal influence is strong. Similarly, the freight market often suffers during years of strong metal and water.

This phenomenon is not difficult to understand if one remembers the much-used example of Mr. Li Ka-shing. I have explained earlier that people are destined to go into a certain trade, not because the trade is his favourite element, but because he possesses an excessive amount of such an element in his destiny. Therefore, a person may enter the shipping line because his destiny possesses excessive water and metal elements. Water and metal are unfavourable elements to him, and he needs wood and fire to counter the excessive metal and water. Thus, a metal and water year will not bring prosperity to this shipping man. This is why we often find the freight market stronger not in years of water and metal, but in years of wood and fire.

All Businesses Need *Feng Shui* To Prosper

The Four Pillars of Destiny is a very handy tool in assisting our business decisions. Readers who wish to learn more about the technique can refer to the appendices at the end of this book. They can also refer to my other books.

But despite its great success in evaluating human fortune, the Four Pillars of Destiny is still a somewhat passive metaphysical art. In theory, we can adjust and focus our direction in life better and be quicker in seizing opportunities if we understands our self potential and the cycle of ups and downs. This can be regarded as a positive aspect of learning the Four Pillars of Destiny. But the art itself does not provide any active means for us to improve our future or to enhance our potential. For example, if a person realises that he will be in good fortune to earn money in a particular year, as revealed by his Four Pillars of Destiny, what can he do to enhance and maximise his potential gains? The art of the Four Pillars of Destiny does not offer the means to increase his gains from ten thousand to one million. To supplement for this drawback, the Chinese have another metaphysical tool called *feng shui* which is believed to be able to change the level of our gains or losses.

Let me demonstrate with an example. In this book, I have frequently used Mr. Li Ka-shing's destiny as a typical example of a wealthy man. However, many boys were born at the same time as Mr. Li Ka-shing. In other words, there are other people with exactly the same Four Pillars of Destiny as Mr. Li. Yet, we are only aware that Mr. Li is a property tycoon. What about the others? Why didn't they become property tycoons like Mr. Li? Besides the pillars of destiny, other factors must be at play to bring about the great success of Mr. Li. The third factor, besides the influence of destiny and luck—as I have mentioned in the opening chapter of this book—is *feng shui*. *Feng shui* is believed to be the force which can influence human destiny. It is a factor which will enhance good destiny if applied wisely. As Mr. Li was destined to become a rich man, without the assistance of *feng shui*, he could still have become a millionaire. With the support of good *feng shui*, his wealth multiplied and today, he is much more than just a millionaire.

What Is *Feng Shui*?

So what exactly is this *feng shui* which is able to influence our destiny? It is a unique subject in Chinese metaphysics dealing with the influence of the environment on human fortune. The subject is an entirely different branch of metaphysics, distinct from the Four Pillars of Destiny. The four pillars cover the aspect of human fortune and destiny. *Feng shui* is a study of the living environment, which includes our earth, the landscape, the sea, the rivers and the houses in which man takes shelter. Traditional Chinese believe that man is a member of the universe and is thus very much influenced by the universe in our daily lives. The universe is our environment and we are intimately affected by the forces of nature existing in our environment. Such forces of nature are able to affect our destiny.

Before I proceed to explain *feng shui* in more detail, I have to resolve the eternal question—can destiny be changed? This introduction on *feng shui* forces may appear to impress upon readers that destiny can be changed. But it seems paradoxical because if destiny can be changed, it is not foreseeable and all the theories of the Four Pillars of Destiny will break down. To resolve this paradox, we should view *feng shui* as a tool to modify the standard of our destiny. The Four Pillars of Destiny allow us to see our potential and fortune profile. We can then predict our ups and downs in advance. However, the intensity of the ups and downs will be affected by factors other than destiny. *Feng shui* is one of these factors—others being freewill, philanthropy and effort. As such, I believe that *feng shui* will not change the shape of our fortune profile already defined in our destiny, but *feng shui* can change the intensity and the degree of the ups and downs. With good *feng shui*, our up cycle will become even more prosperous and our suffering in the down cycle will lessen. But *feng shui* cannot reverse a low point into prosperity.

With a clear understanding of the relationship between destiny and *feng shui*, let me now explain *feng shui* in more detail. First let me explain what *feng shui* is. Literally the two words simply mean wind and water. We believe that these two words originated from an ancient book called the "Rules for Burial" which contained the following sentence: "The flow of energy dissipated by wind and stops at the boundary of water."

The "energy" mentioned here is not clear in meaning but we believe it refers to some abstract natural forces which flow with the landscape and have effect on people. And so it is called a *feng shui* force. As *feng shui* is some abstract force relating to the landscape and can influence the human wellbeing, I would define the subject simply as one which studies the environmental influence on human fortune. The emphasis is on fortune so as to differentiate the subject from other kinds of social or economic studies about the environment. Therefore, *feng shui* is some force of nature which exists in our environment and will cast good or bad effects on our fortune. The objective of *feng shui* study is to find ways to make use of the good influences and to avoid the bad influences in our environment.

There are two types of *feng shui* environments. One is physical, referring to the actual, visible surroundings. Examples would be the landscape, mountains, rivers, buildings, roads, the interior design and layout of our house or even a seemingly minor object placed on our desk. Each item is believed to cast some *feng shui* influence on us. The second type, more mysterious and abstract, is the directional influences, which are invisible, but have an impact on human fortune according to direction and time. When evaluating *feng shui* influences, it is absolutely necessary to take both types into consideration. For example, most Chinese palaces and temples are built with red walls with sharp edges on the roof. Red is regarded as the colour of fire and sharp pointed objects are considered the shape of fire. So the physical outlook of such a building reflects an image of fire and is susceptible to fire disasters. But not all Chinese palaces burned down. The reason is that the physical shape alone, without interacting with any intangible directional influences, cannot cause a fire to occur. A fire only occurs when certain directional influences associated with the fire element arrive at such a building.

If we look back on the history of the Forbidden City—the famous Chinese palace in Beijing—we see that a large number of fire disasters occurred within the city. And each time, the city was found to have been influenced by the fire element of the directional forces.

What are these directional forces? They are a subject of much speculation. Some say they are magnetic waves; others associate them with cosmic rays and energy. To date, there has not been any organised scientific study to ascertain its true nature. However, the ancient Chinese seem to have discovered a pattern to trace their influences, so that they can predict their movement and develop theories to use or control these mysterious forces.

How they managed to acquire such knowledge is a mystery. But it is believed that the knowledge and technique emerged from a solid foundation of Chinese metaphysical views about the universe and nature. It will be overly ambitious to try to fully explain the whole body of the Chinese metaphysical system behind the directional *feng shui* influences. However, I can still present to you a brief outline of the major theories behind the dynamic *feng shui* system.

Let us briefly examine these theories individually. As the study of *feng shui* is about the effect of nature or the environment on human fortune, a complete theory of *feng shui* must comprise at least three aspects: firstly, an understanding of nature or the universe, secondly, a concept of time, and finally, a concept of space.

The Concept Of The Universe And Nature

The ancient Chinese have long formulated a set of theories about nature. Basically, they have discovered the dualism of yin and yang. To everything, there exists the yang, or the positive, the male, the bright side, and the opposite is yin, or the negative, the female, the dark side. These two aspects are complementary and are integral to each other. Harmony can only be achieved with a balance between the yang and yin. Such belief is clearly reflected in the "Tai Chi" diagram which shows the black and white sides of a circle merging into each other. Such philosophy is fundamental to Chinese culture.

Fig. 2 The Tai Chi showing yin and yang

Next comes the theory of the five basic elements which I have already introduced in the previous chapters about the Four Pillars of Destiny. The ancient Chinese believed everything in the universe is composed of and subject to five basic forces or kinds of energies. They are symbolised by the five kinds of matters which we commonly find on earth. These are Metal, Wood, Water, Fire and Earth. The metaphysical belief is that every picce of matter, material or abstract, including man and his fortunes, can be represented by such elements and are subject to the influence of these elements. The ancient Chinese then took another step further to establish the relationship among these five elements in the form of two basic rules. These rules are the Cycle of Birth and the Cycle of Destruction shown again below:

Fig. 3 The Cycle of Birth

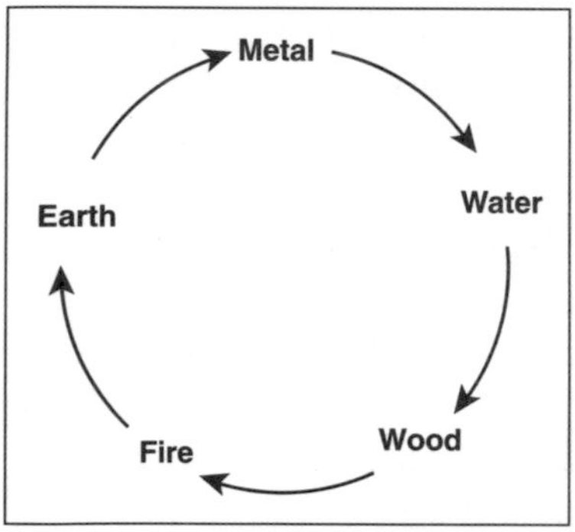

Fig. 4 The Cycle of Destruction

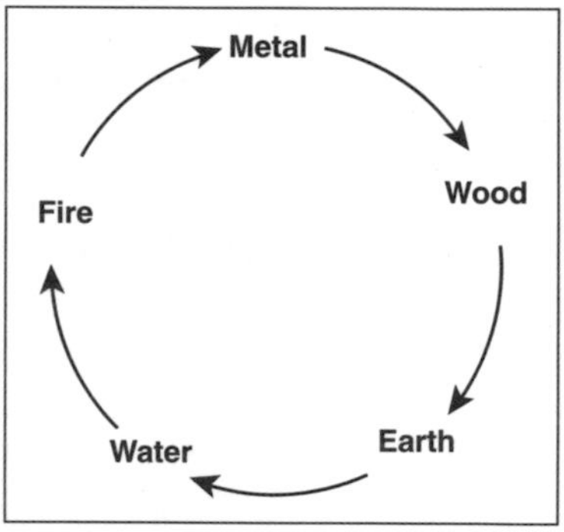

The concept of yin and yang and the two cycles of the five elements are considered the fundamental rules of nature and are applied in all Chinese metaphysical studies.

It is believed that the theory of yin and yang and the five elements form the background of the ancient book of I Ching, or the "Book of Change". This book is regarded by many as the book which reveals the wisdom and understanding of the ancient Chinese about the universe. The book's author and origin is unknown and its original form contained only eight trigrams, each in the form of three broken or continuous lines. A broken line reflects the yin aspect of matter and the continuous line reflects the yang aspect. By putting broken and continuous lines in combinations of three, we have altogether eight different combinations called the "Eight Trigrams".

Each Trigram is assigned various meanings, including a basic element, a member in a family, a natural phenomenon, an animal, even a season, a body organ or a class of people. In short, it is intended to symbolise everything in the universe. By combining any two of these trigrams at random, we can obtain a total of 64 hexagrams each with six lines. And these 64 hexagrams provide more detailed representation of matters and complicated human relationships. The I Ching, as we know it today, is a book consisting of detailed explanations of these 64 hexagrams, complied by Confucius and the Emperor of the Chou Dynasty. This book can be consulted on all matters and has been used for oracle purposes by the Chinese for thousands of years. More discussion about the I Ching Oracle can be found in later chapters of this book.

Fig. 5 The Eight Trigrams

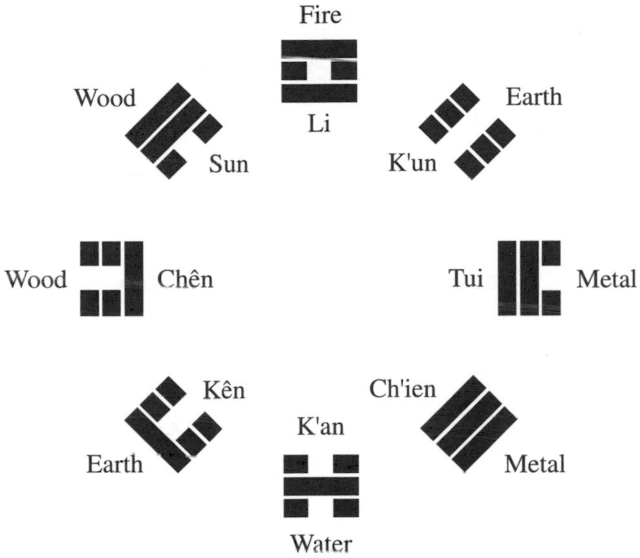

Fire
Li
Wood
Sun
Earth
K'un
Wood
Chên
Tui
Metal
Kên
Earth
K'an
Water
Ch'ien
Metal

The Concept Of Time

Besides knowledge of the universe and the rules of nature, we also need a clear concept of time. The universe is not static and its natural influence will change over time. This is one point I need to emphasize. *Feng shui* will change over time and no good *feng shui* can last forever. As we can observe in Chinese history, dynasties, over the centuries, prospered and declined and no dynasty has lasted to this day. A proper *feng shui* theory must then incorporate the time element and be able to trace the pattern of change over time.

The *feng shui* system divides time into cycles of 180 years. One cycle consists of three periods of 60 years and each period consists of three ages of 20 years. The 20 years from 1984 to 2003 is the Age of Seven, under the

Lower Period. This concept of age holds much significance in the Flying Star *feng shui* method which I have adopted for this book. Before we can inspect the *feng shui* of a house, we need to know what age the house was completed under. It is worthwhile remembering that houses completed between 1984 and 2003 are called "Age of Seven houses" in *feng shui* terminology.

Fig. 6 The Three Periods and Nine Ages

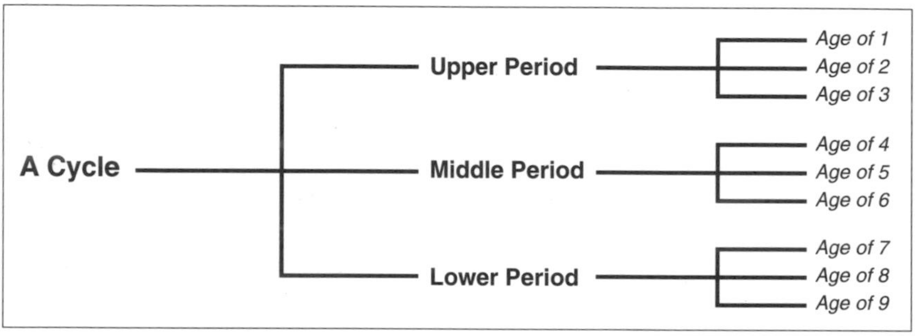

- **A Cycle**
  - **Upper Period**
    - *Age of 1*
    - *Age of 2*
    - *Age of 3*
  - **Middle Period**
    - *Age of 4*
    - *Age of 5*
    - *Age of 6*
  - **Lower Period**
    - *Age of 7*
    - *Age of 8*
    - *Age of 9*

The Concept Of Space

Armed with a basic concept of time and the universe, we still need a concept of space before we can construct a firm foundation for a complete *feng shui* theory. This idea of space was inspired by a mysterious diagram called the Lo Shu which was first discovered on the back of a giant tortoise that emerged from the river Lo in central China about 6,000 years ago. Figure 7 is a reproduction of the original Lo Shu diagram.

Fig. 7 The Lo Shu diagram

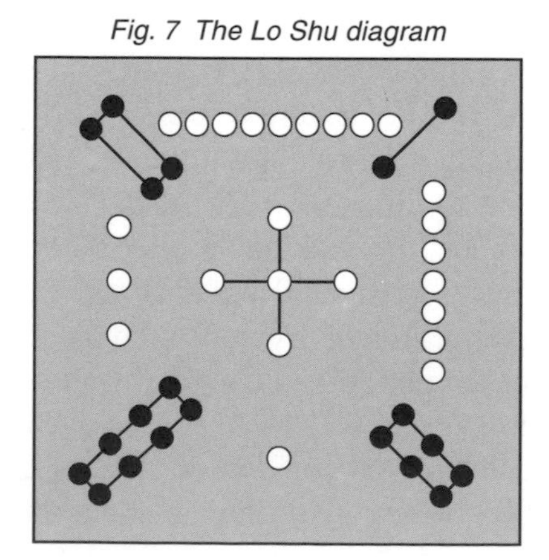

Fig. 8 The Lo Shu expressed in numbers

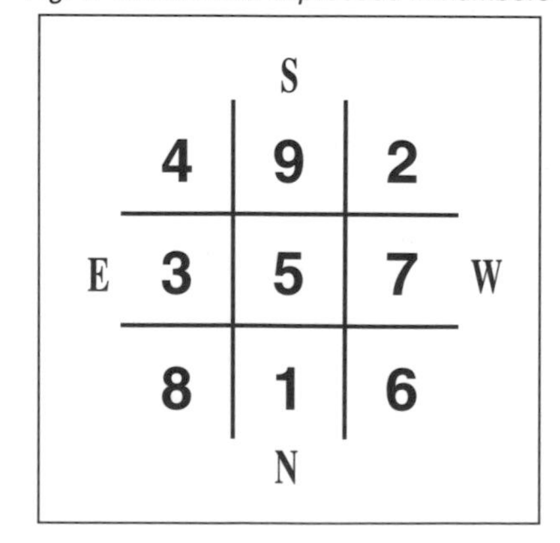

This diagram, for convenience sake, is often drawn in the form of a nine square chart with each square representing a direction. Inside each square, we place a number to represent the dots in the original Lo Shu diagram. This magic nine square chart is called the original Lo Shu diagram and is the foundation for the body of *feng shui* theories generally applied by geomancers today. The numbers in each square symbolise a type of *feng shui* influence present in a certain direction. Observe that no matter how you add up any three numbers in straight lines or across, you always get the sum of 15.

I have emphasized to readers that the Flying Star school of *feng shui* is dynamic in the sense that it incorporates the time element. In the same way, the Lo Shu diagram, represented by the nine square chart, changes with time. The numbers inside each square are dynamic and move in a fixed pattern. If the centre number is replaced, the other numbers automatically change position in the same pattern. If we start counting from the number 5 in the centre of the square, we can detect the following pattern of movement:

Centre	NW	W	NE	S	N	SW	E	SE
5	6	7	8	9	1	2	3	4

The greatest significance of this nine square chart is that it reveals to us the pattern of movement of the *feng shui* forces as time changes. So the numbers in each square embraces many meanings. Each number represents a Trigram of the I Ching; hence all the hidden meanings of a Trigram are incorporated. Each also bears a basic element and possess the yin and yang character. Furthermore, as mentioned earlier, time is divided in nine Ages of 20 years each. Thus the numbers also symbolise Ages. The following table briefly summarises the meanings of the numbers from 1 to 9:

Number	Trigram	Element	Nature	Person	Age
1	☵	Water	Water	Middle-aged man	1
2	☷	Earth	Earth	Old woman	2
3	☳	Wood	Thunder	Eldest son	3
4	☴	Wood	Wind	Eldest daughter	4
5	–	Earth	–	–	5
6	☰	Metal	Heaven	Old man	6
7	☱	Metal	Swamp	Young girl	7
8	☶	Earth	Mountain	Young boy	8
9	☲	Fire	Fire	Middle-aged woman	9

The number 5 is regarded as the controlling and balancing power in the centre. It does not belong to any trigram and does not carry any meaning like the other numbers.

Observe that the nine square chart derived from the Lo Shu diagram incorporates all the theories I mentioned before. It embraces the rules of nature, the five basic elements and, in addition, also indicates how the forces of nature change with time in a fixed pattern. The numbers in the diagram are dynamic as they move from Age to Age, year to year, month to month, even day to day, according to the pattern shown in the table. The changes are initiated by altering the number in the centre. For example, to find the *feng shui* forces present in different directions during the Age of Seven (1984–2003), we put the number 7 in the middle square and place the consecutive numbers 8 and 9 around it. We then return to place the remaining numbers 1, 2, 3, 4, 5 and 6 into the remaining 6 squares according to the Lo Shu pattern. Finally we obtain a new nine square chart as shown below, which reveals the *feng shui* influence during the Age of Seven.

Fig. 9 Feng shui chart for Age of Seven

		S		
	6	2	4	
E	5	7	9	W
	1	3	8	
		N		

It is worthwhile familiarising ourselves with these nine square charts as they form the basis for detecting the directional *feng shui* influences affecting buildings. Given the Age of a building along with its direction, we can immediately draw up a nine square chart showing the intangible forces affecting from all directions. This is called the *feng shui* or "Flying Star" chart of the building. If we take one step further and compare the directional influences of a certain year or month with the Flying Star chart of the building, we can see how the numbers, or Flying Stars, interact with one another. It is by this method that we can assess the fortune of a building and predict events.

This technique of the "Flying Star School" of *feng shui* was a well-kept secret of the ancient Chinese. Rediscovered during the Ching Dynasty, it has since become the most popular and practical method among *feng shui* experts today.

Learning the technique will not be easy. However, readers will find it rewarding to try to understand its workings as its theories can be applied to enhance the profitability and prosperity of your business ventures.

ESSENTIAL *FENG SHUI* TECHNIQUES FOR MANAGERS

In the last chapter, I introduced many *feng shui* terms. Some are very abstract and are not easy to grasp. To enable readers to gain a better understanding of the subject, let us go on a field trip where we can conduct a practical exercise in *feng shui* analysis.

Assuming I receive a request to inspect the *feng shui* of a residential house. The first step, before taking the field trip, is to collect some background information. One essential piece of information a *feng shui* practitioner requires is the age of the building. As mentioned in the last chapter, time is divided into ages of 20 years. For instance, a building constructed and completed in the period between 1964 to 1983 (inclusive) is called an Age of Six building. Its *feng shui* influence is totally different from that of a building completed before or after that age, even though they both sit on the same site, facing the same direction.

Another piece of information we usually require is the birth data of the residents of the house. This data is used in several ways. Firstly, people born under different years receive different *feng shui* influences and it is essential to determine if there is any *feng shui* conflict between the residents' birth data and the direction of the house. Secondly, the birth data can be used to help select the best colour scheme and decorations for the house, and to choose the most suitable sleeping locations for the residents. In this latter respect, we are, in fact, dealing with the technique of the Four Pillars of Destiny. Besides collecting data about the house and the dwellers, the client should also advise the *feng shui* practitioner of any special reasons for requesting a *feng shui* analysis so that the practitioner can focus on problem areas.

Tools For *Feng Shui* Fieldwork

Before taking the field trip, let us carefully check all the necessary tools. There are not many items needed for *feng shui* field work—the most indispensable instrument is the Lo Pan, the Chinese *feng shui* compass. In the simplest terms, it is a compass with a magnetic needle for measuring directions. Unlike common compasses, however, it includes numerous concentric rings, each showing complicated trigrams, stars, heavenly stems, earthly branches and numbers. Do not be put off by its apparent complexity as most of the symbols are only used in selecting grave sites, or yin houses. To analyse the *feng shui* of yang houses (houses for the living), beginners need only to be familiar with the ring called the 24 mountains. This comprises 360 degrees divided into 24 sections, with each section occupying 15 degrees.

Fig. 10 The 24 mountains of the Lo Pan

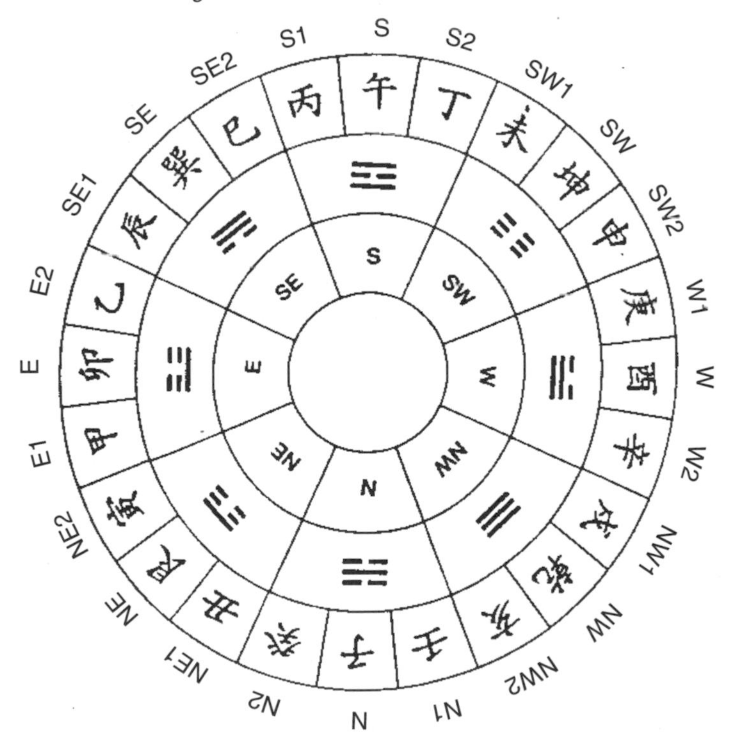

Besides the compass, I usually carry a booklet called *The Thousand Years Almanac*. This is used for converting the Western calendar into the Chinese. I also use another measuring device, usually a sonic ruler, to measure the dimensions of a house so that floor plans can be drawn to scale.

Establishing Directions

I have emphasised in the last chapter that there are two aspects to *feng shui*, the physical environment and the intangible influences. The first step in inspecting a building is to walk around the site to observe its physical surroundings and to establish its directions. Deciding on a building's direction is very important as this is an essential step in drawing up its *feng shui* chart. Any error made at this stage may render the entire *feng shui* analysis worthless or worse, misleading. In the old days, it was easy to establish the front and back of a building as most buildings were of rectangular shape with the front entrance usually representing the direction of the building. However, modern buildings, especially skyscrapers, can come in very irregular shapes and may require some very skilful judgement to determine the front and the back. Years of experience and a solid theoretical foundation may be required to form a good judgement.

Having established the direction of a building, we can then use the Lo Pan to accurately measure directional bearings. When measuring, I always try to stand as far away from the building as possible, in an unobstructed open space, as the concrete mass of a huge building and any metal objects nearby will affect the magnetic needle of the compass and lead to inaccurate readings. For the same reason, I never trust the compass once I enter a building as the readings inside a house are affected by furniture and fixtures. Using the age of the house and the directional readings, we can now draw up a *feng shui* chart in the nine square format showing all the influences the building will receive from all directions. After completing this preparatory work, we are ready to inspect the flat inside the building.

Inspecting The Interior

On entering the flat, we should ascertain in which part of the building it is located and what its relative direction is. Then we can inspect the entire flat to get an idea of its general layout and draw up a floor plan. Figures 11 and 12 show a sample floor plan of a flat and the corresponding *feng shui* chart showing its directional influences. The large number in the centre is 6, indicating that this building was constructed in the Age of Six (1964 to 1983 inclusive). The small pairs of numbers in each square are *feng shui* influences, commonly called "flying stars". The numbers on the left, called "mountain stars", affect human prosperity or health while the numbers on the right, called "water stars", govern financial prosperity.

Fig. 11 Sample floor plan of a flat

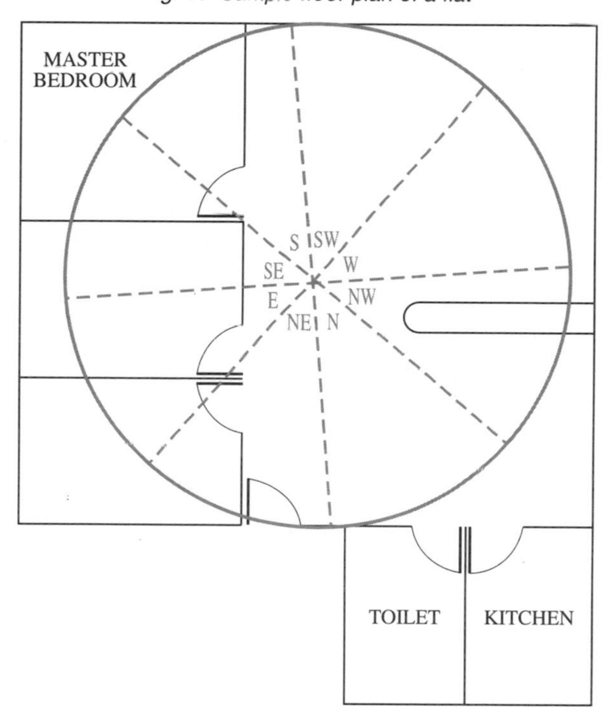

Fig. 12 Feng shui chart of the sample flat

			SW
	8 2 **5**	4 7 **1**	6 9 **3**
	7 1 **4**	9 3 **6**	2 5 **8**
	3 6 **9**	5 8 **2**	1 4 **7**
NE			

With a floor plan of the flat in one hand and the *feng shui* chart of the building in the other, a *feng shui* expert can begin analysing the positive and negative aspects of the whole building and how its surroundings and intangible forces affect its financial and human prosperity. The same *feng shui* chart for the building can also be applied to describe the *feng shui* prosperity of the flat inside. The essential point to note is the location of the main entrance, as all good or bad influences enter through the front door. Equally important is the location of the master bedroom which very much affects the health and prosperity of the household.

For example, the main entrance to the flat in Figure 11 is located in the northeast. The corresponding *feng shui* chart shows the numbers 3 and 6 in this location. This means that the front entrance of the flat is subject to the influence of *feng shui* forces represented by these two stars. As the entrance is a location of activity, a mobile and fluid place, the major emphasis is on the water star which, in this case, is 6. This star belongs to the past Age of Six. Because we are now in the Age of Seven, it symbolises faded prosperity and is thus not a beneficial star. We can conclude that the entrance is not favourably located to admit financial prosperity.

The small numbers in the flying star chart—the water stars and mountain stars—are symbols of various *feng shui* influences acting upon a house at different locations. Each number carries profound meanings that are basically derived from the trigram of the I Ching. By examining the numbers present in a direction of the nine square flying star chart, we can gain a insight into the degree of prosperity or misfortune occurring in a particular location of a house as represented by a square of the chart. Accurate interpretation of the meanings of these small numbers is essential in the *feng shui* analysis of a house. The table opposite summarises the essential implications of each of these numbers in the flying star chart of a house:

No.	Trigram	Element	Person	Object	Body	Effects
1		Water	Middle-aged man	Den, Blood	Ear, Kidney	Academic Matters
2		Earth	Old woman	Earth, Ox	Nose, Stomach	Sickness
3		Wood	Eldest son	Thunder	Foot, Hair, Liver	Anger
4		Wood	Eldest daughter	Wind, Rope	Buttocks, Neck	Romance, Sex
5	—	Earth	—	Shar	—	Bad luck, Obstacles
6		Metal	Old man	Heaven	Head, Lungs	Past prosperity, Legal matters
7		Metal	Young girl	Lake	Mouth	Current prosperity
8		Earth	Young boy	Mountain	Hands	Coming prosperity
9		Fire	Middle-aged woman	Beauty	Eyes, Heart	Future prosperity

A good *feng shui* expert will thoroughly comment on the location of every major room in an apartment, as well as the placement of the more important furniture and decorative objects, such as beds, tables, stoves, television sets and telephones, and explain in detail how the floor layout and the position of each object affects the prosperity of the house. Besides the interior decoration, he will also explain how the outside surroundings affect your home. All this information goes hand in hand with his analysis of the birth data of the residents, which judges their compatibility with the house and determines suitable colour schemes and decor.

Dynamic Influences

I have emphasised several times that *feng shui* reading is dynamic as its influence changes over time. Thus the *feng shui* master will look some months into the future and inform the household what they should be prepared for. For example, if the inauspicious star of yellow 5 is expected to arrive in the front entrance during a particular month, the expert may tell the household to hang a wind chime at the front entrance during that month to dissolve the bad influence.

Returning to our example, the *feng shui* chart shown in Figure 12 only shows the static *feng shui* influence of the building. There are also yearly, monthly and even daily *feng shui* influences which will interact with the static *feng shui* chart of the building to cause and influence events. These yearly, monthly and daily *feng shui* forces, or flying stars, move in the same pattern as the Lo Shu diagram discussed in the last chapter, and can also be expressed in a nine square chart. Figure 13 shows such a flying star chart reflecting the influences in the month of November 1992.

Fig. 13 Flying star chart for November 1992

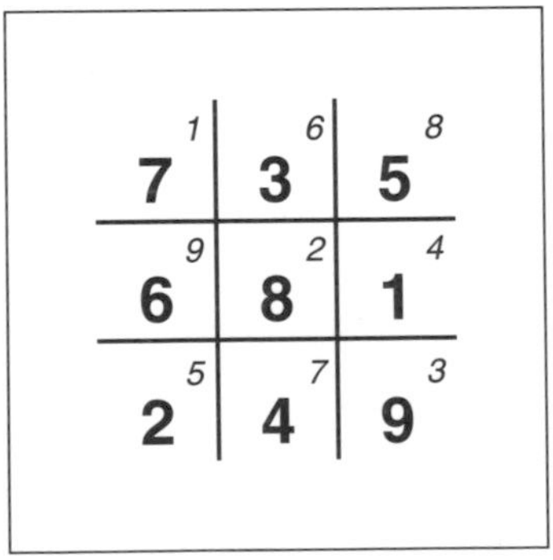

7^{1}	3^{6}	5^{8}
6^{9}	8^{2}	1^{4}
2^{5}	4^{7}	9^{3}

By superimposing this monthly star chart onto the static *feng shui* chart of the building, we can see the yearly star 2 (the larger number) and monthly star 5 (the smaller number) arrived at the northeast location in November 1992. This is the location of the main entrance to the flat. As the star 5 symbolises trouble and the star 2 represents sickness, it is not surprising to learn that the head of the household of this flat was indeed hospitalised in November of that year.

Before leaving the house, the *feng shui* expert will give his view of the house and make recommendations for measures which should be taken to ward off future threats to prosperity. It is also my practice to make detailed measurements of the house so I can draw up a floor plan to scale. This is essential to reconfirm which sector of a house comes under which directional *feng shui* influence. A rough sketch of the floor plan is usually not accurate enough for a detailed interpretation.

The last step is to prepare a full report for the client, recording all comments and explanations, illustrated with drawings and recommendations. Again I consider this an essential step. It not only provides the client with clear instructions of what changes are required, but also gives the *feng shui* expert a complete record of previous assignments should the same client have follow-up requests in the future.

By now, readers should possess a general idea of what *feng shui* is and what a *feng shui* expert is expected to do when providing a service. If readers wish to go deeper into the technical aspects and conduct their own experiments, a knowledge of how to draw up *feng shui* charts and interpret the stars is needed. The formulae behind the making of these charts are presented at the end of this book as an appendix—they will enable readers to draw up charts for buildings of all ages.

The proper interpretation of these charts require deeper knowledge and experience. This is best conveyed as I lead you through some real life examples included in the following chapters.

At the end of this book there is another appendix listing out the 17 vital steps needed to evaluate the *feng shui* of a house. If readers are familiar with these steps, we can move on to the business environment to see how we can make full use of these *feng shui* tools to enhance our business prosperity and to avoid the danger of bad *feng shui* influence.

Choosing A Prosperous Office Building

The most useful application of *feng shui* principles in business is in the selection and interior arrangement of the business premises to enhance prosperity. Many commercial buildings in Hong Kong, Taiwan and Singapore are believed to have been designed with the participation of *feng shui* experts, and the prosperity of some well-known organisations in the Orient is attributed to the good *feng shui* design of their office buildings.

The Hongkong And Shanghai Bank Building

A prominent example in Hong Kong is the famous Hongkong and Shanghai Bank Building in the Central District. Its location is believed to be a dragon's den of the Victoria Peak. The Chinese believe mountain ranges are like dragons with very strong natural forces and the dragon's den is the spot where the massive benevolent forces of the dragon concentrates. The Hongkong Bank Building sitting in such a den is able to absorb the natural forces to enhance its prosperity. A dragon's den also requires a special configuration of the surrounding landscape or environment to keep the benevolent forces in. Otherwise, the good influence will dissipate rapidly.

In this respect, the site of the Hongkong Bank possesses all the guards and shields which satisfy the criteria. On its left and right, there are the Standard Chartered Bank Building and the old Bank of China Building, acting as the dragon's arm and the tiger's arm (meaning guards on the left and right), respectively. In front of the Hongkong Bank is Statue Square, which is called the bright hall, to hold the benevolent forces. Beyond Statue Square is the Star Ferry Pier and the City Hall Building to act as a shield. An important criteria for the *feng shui* forces to stop and concentrate is water. There is a famous ancient saying that "the natural forces will dissipate by wind, but stop at the boundary of water". Here, the Victoria Harbour in front of the Bank serves this purpose exactly.

So the Hongkong Bank enjoys an ideal *feng shui* environment. However, as mentioned in the previous chapter, a good physical environment alone cannot guarantee good *feng shui*. We also need to look at the intangible forces. To assess the influence of the intangible forces, it is necessary to measure the direction of the Hongkong Bank Building and to ascertain the age of the building. With these two pieces of information, we can draw up a *feng shui* chart showing the major *feng shui* influences from all directions.

The present Hongkong Bank Building was completed after the year 1984, making it an Age of Seven building. It sits in a south-north direction. The following chart shows the intangible forces affecting each direction of the building:

Fig. 14 The feng shui environment of the Hongkong Bank

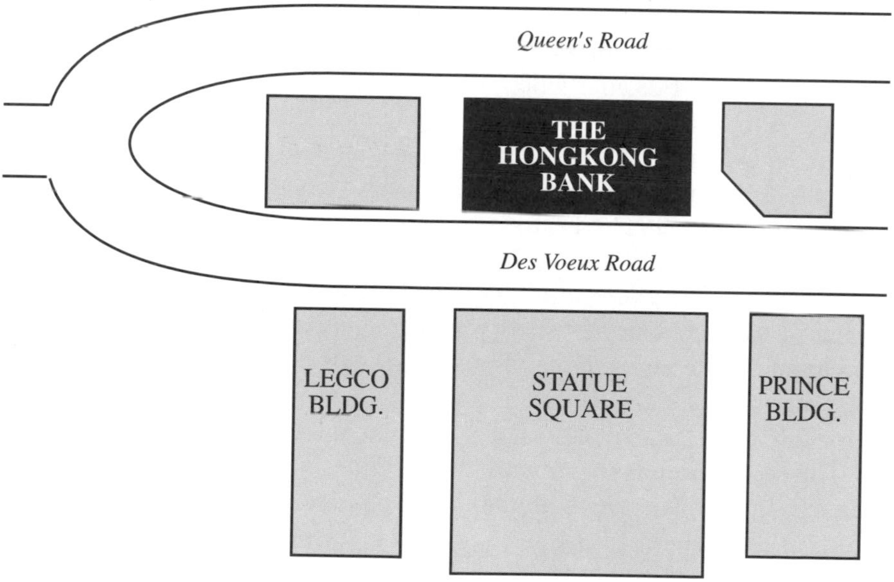

Fig. 15 The feng shui chart of the Hongkong Bank

S

1 4 **6**	6 8 **2**	8 6 **4**
9 5 **5**	2 3 **7**	4 1 **9**
5 9 **1**	7 7 **3**	3 2 **8**

N

Each square of the chart represents a direction. The front of the building faces north, so it is represented by the lowermost square marked N. There are three numbers in this square. The small number 7 on the right represents a water star, affecting money prosperity while the small number 7 on the left represents a mountain star, affecting human prosperity and harmony. The larger number 3 is derived from the Age of Seven and is of less importance at this stage.

When interpreting these *feng shui* charts, one must always bear in mind two major principles. Firstly, as we are in the Age of Seven between the years 1984 and 2003, the most prosperous number is 7. The second best number is 8, as 8 is the age that follows immediately, while 9 is third best. By the same token, numbers smaller than 7 are bad numbers as they represent past ages and, therefore, bad influences. Hence, the first step when interpreting a *feng shui* chart is to see where the small numbers 7 and 8 are. In the chart, there are always two 7s and two 8s, as they can be either mountain stars or water stars, depending on their left or right positions on the chart. Water stars affect money prosperity while mountain stars affect human health and harmony. In our example of the Hongkong Bank, we can see that both the water star 7 and the mountain star 7 are in the north, the water star 8 is in the south while the mountain star 8 is found in the southwest.

The second step is to compare the locations of these prosperous mountain stars and water stars with the actual physical environment. We should examine the features of the area where the prosperous stars of 7 and 8 are located. Always remember that for the prosperous stars to act, a prosperous mountain star must be located on a mountain while a prosperous water star must be located in water. In modern cities, mountains and waters are not always available so we can extend the term mountain to embrace buildings, tall structures, higher ground and quiet and enclosed areas such as a room. For water, the term also includes low ground, an open space such as a garden, roads, mobile areas such as the entrance or doorway and areas of activity such as the living room and conference room. If the water stars 7 and 8 are found at the entrance or in an open space, they will enhance money prosperity. Similarly, if the mountain stars 7 and 8 are found in the location of tall buildings, they will enhance human harmony.

Armed with this knowledge, let us examine the *feng shui* chart of the Hongkong Bank. We find the water star 7 in the north which is exactly the front direction of the building. In front of the building, we see the entrance, the Statue Square, Queen's Road and the Victoria Harbour which all fall under the "water" category. So money prosperity for the Bank is assured. Another prosperous water star 8 is found in the south, where the bank has a back entrance and a road. Again, this will enhance prosperity, not only in the Age of Seven but also over the next 20 years in the Age of Eight. Thus the two entrances, one in the north and the other in the south, will guarantee prosperity for the bank until, at least, the year 2023—the end of the Age of Eight.

Now let us look at the mountain stars. The mountain star 7 is in the north where there are no tall buildings. So the configuration for human harmony is not as good as for money prosperity. However, beyond the Victoria Harbour, there are tall mountains on the Kowloon side which somewhat remedies this drawback. The mountain star 8 is found in the southwest where we can find tall buildings and the Victoria Peak. We can thus expect better human harmony in the bank in the Age of Eight after the year 2003.

The above is a simple example of how to assess the prosperity of an office building. This is the first step to finding prosperous premises where we can buy an office unit or a shop site to take up a business venture. However, I have to caution readers that modern buildings house many units or flats and each unit has a different interior arrangement. Therefore, a prosperous building does not automatically mean all units within the same building will be prosperous. As we can see from the *feng shui* chart of the Hongkong Bank, the small numbers 5 are found in the east and northeast. These are bad *feng shui* influences and an office located in these corners, if not well designed to enhance the prosperous stars 7 and 8, may not share the prosperity of the building. Hence, it is essential that we not only select a good building, but also a good unit within the building. The latter is, in fact, even more important than the former.

Selecting a prosperous building is essential if you are doing a retail business where what you need is not an office but a retail shop in an arcade. In this case, the prosperity of the building will ensure the popularity of the arcade and the shop.

Shapes That Reduce Prosperity

There are also other *feng shui* considerations regarding the physical environment of the building. Some structures of special shapes are believed to bring bad influence to a building and reduce its prosperity. Such objects are called physical "shars" and should be avoided as far as possible. The following are some common examples:

• Sharp pointed objects. Sharp edges facing a building are considered a physical shar (objects which cause bad *feng shui* influence). One controversial building in Hong Kong is the new Bank of China Building which is triangular in shape with many sharp edges on its upper levels.

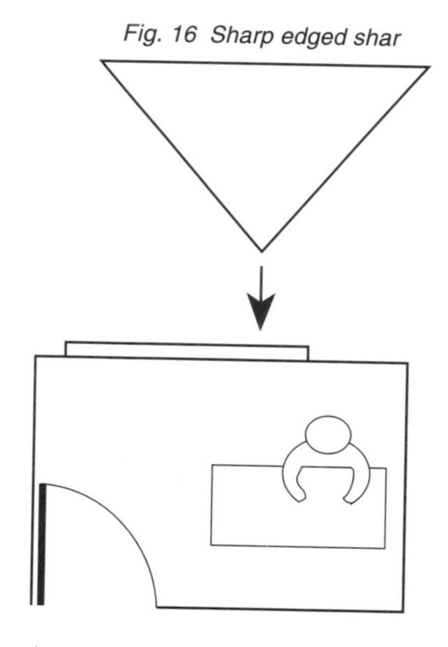

Fig. 16 Sharp edged shar

• A curved blade. A road or a flyover with the curved edge facing a building is considered bad *feng shui* as it symbolises the blade of a sword cutting through a building. However, a road with its curve embracing or surrounding a building is considered a beneficial configuration.

Fig. 17 Curved blade shar

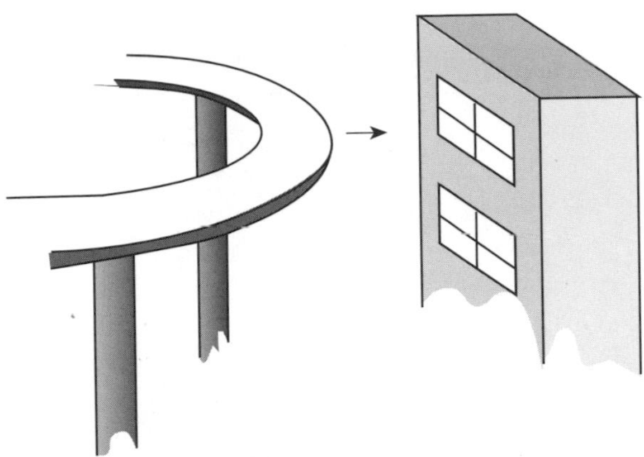

• A flat top. On looking out the window, if the roof of a nearby building is at the same level as your floor, it is considered a flat top shar. One explanation for this shar is that the wind and current will be strongest on the roof top level of the nearby building.

Fig. 18 Flat top shar

• Crack from the sky. This is a configuration of two neighbouring tall buildings, separated only by a narrow lane. The resulting appearance is that of a large crack in between two tall structures. The explanation is similar to the flat top shar above, with the wind and current appearing to be strongest at the "crack".

Fig. 19 Crack from the sky

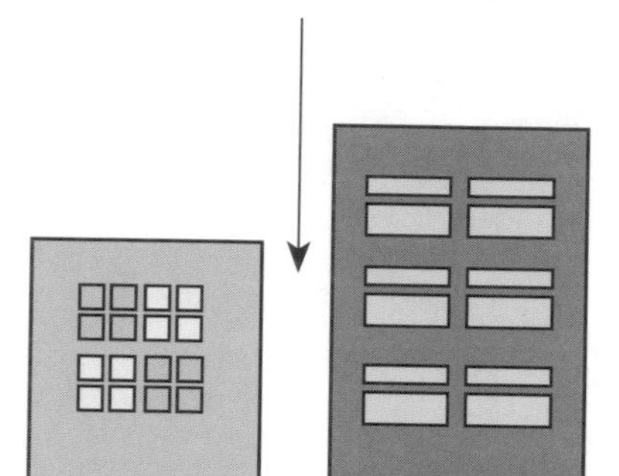

• A peeping building. This term refers to two neighbouring buildings, one in front of the other, but with the one behind slightly higher. The configuration resembles a man hiding behind the shorter building, peeping at you and is a symbol of theft.

Fig. 20 Peeping shar

• Tiger's head. If you look out the window of your building, you may see some concrete structures on the roof tops of shorter buildings. These are structures supporting the lift or water tank. These protruding structures, combined with bad *feng shui* forces, can cause mishaps and are called t gers' heads.

Fig. 21 Tiger's head

• The lonely building. This is a building much higher than its surrounding and is not a good configuration, being subject to strong wind with little protection or shelter. It can be compared to a lonely man standing on a mountain top.

Fig. 22 Lonely building

• Water cutting the feet. A building standing right at the water front with little space between the foot of the building and the sea is not a good configuration. Neither is a building standing on the edge of a cliff. Both symbolise the lack of a strong foundation.

Fig. 23 Water cutting the feet

• Buildings of a special nature. Buildings that serve a special purpose may have some effect on the *feng shui* of the environment. The effect mainly follows the nature of the building. For example, a police station is said to be related to violence as firearms and criminals are present. A temple, on the other hand, may absorb the beneficial influences in the environment, leaving little prosperity for the other nearby buildings. Other special sites such as prisons, hospitals, funeral parlours and graveyards are associated with sorrow and misfortune and are not considered as happy neighbours.

These are some common examples of special features in the environment of a building that we should consider when selecting the best location for our business. Some of these physical shars are traditional beliefs and their ill effects are difficult to assess or prove. However, as I have stressed earlier, it takes a combination of both the physical shar and the bad intangible forces to cause misfortune. For example, if your window in the east is facing the sharp edge of the Bank of China building at a close distance, you cannot immediately conclude that this will cause a bad effect. You should first check the *feng shui* chart of your house. If the mountain star in the east square is 7, then you have little to worry about as the tall bank building will enhance the prosperity of the room. On the other hand, you will have a problem if the mountain star in the east is a 5.

FLYING STARS—THE KEY TO SELECTING A GOOD OFFICE

Assuming we have selected a good office building at a prosperous location, the next step is to find the best office unit within the building. Selecting a good office unit is very similar to selecting a good residence, only the emphasis is somewhat different. The objective of an office is profitability, so the emphasis is more on the money aspect whereas for a residence, human health and harmony usually carry more weight.

After selecting a good building in the manner described in the last chapter, we should have the *feng shui* chart of the building. The next step is to apply the *feng shui* chart for each flat or unit to see if the interior arrangements can enhance their prosperity. As water stars govern money prosperity, the prerequisite of a good office is that its entrance and reception area must be in a location where the prosperous water stars 7 or 8 are present. Even if the water stars 7 or 8 cannot be found at the entrance, they should at least be found at the windows so that they can provide prosperity to the office unit.

For example, let's say you are selecting an office unit inside the Hongkong Bank building with the *feng shui* chart illustrated in the last chapter. As the prosperous water star 7 is in the north, facing Statue Square and the Victoria Harbour, in theory, in such building, it is best to select an office unit with its entrance in the north. However, the drawback of such an office is that if the entrance is in the north, the windows will be facing south and so there will not be any seaview. A better choice will be office units with windows facing north to receive the prosperous water star 7 and the entrance at the south to receive the prosperous water star 8. Such an office will have the seaview and still enjoy the prosperity of both the water stars 7 and 8. Offices in this building with the entrance in the east are not a good choice as the water star 5 is located in the east and does not bring prosperity.

A good entrance is the main criterion in selecting a good office unit. But human harmony is also important as we would not want an office often troubled by conflict among staff or between employer and employees, industrial disputes or injuries due to industrial accidents. All these are governed by the mountain stars on the *feng shui* chart.

Human health and harmony can be enhanced by placing a good mountain star of 7 or 8 into a mountain location. Returning to the example of the Hongkong Bank building, the mountain star 8 is in the southwest while the mountain star 7 is in the north. As there are tall buildings southwest of the building and water in the north, placing the chief executive's room in the southwest will help enhance human harmony. So besides getting a prosperous entrance, another point we need to consider is whether the office unit allows the manager's room to be placed in the southwest.

If the office unit satisfies both the above requirements, it is already a good choice. The remaining task is just adding interior decoration to enhance the strength of money and human prosperity, which we will further examine in the next chapter.

The Hongkong Bank is an excellent example of a good *feng shui* building. In practice, good *feng shui* buildings are rare and very expensive. Therefore, for various reasons, such as economic considerations and convenience, we often have to compromise.

How To Make The Best Of What You Have

The following example illustrates how we can choose an office unit from a not so prosperous commercial building. The client is a small property broker who decided to set up his own company after gaining some experience in the trade with a big property enterprise. He can only afford to start in a small office unit of about 100 square feet located in a not so prosperous building in an inexpensive area. The building is new, having been completed in 1993, with its front facing northwest and its back against the southeast. Figure 24 is the *feng shui* chart drawn up for this building.

Fig. 24 Feng shui chart of a commercial building

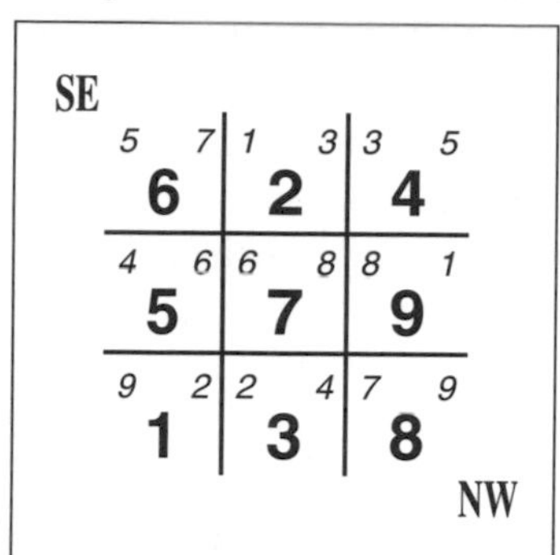

The chart shows that the prosperous water star 7 is in the southeast which is the back of the building. Behind this commercial building is a beautiful playground with much open space. Thus the water star 7 can act to enhance prosperity. It is best to select an office unit not facing the front, but with large windows facing the back, overlooking the playground. The window will let in the prosperity of the water star 7. My client was able to select a small office unit with such a window facing southeast. Figure 25 shows the location of his office in relation to the commercial building and the sketch of his interior layout.

Fig. 25 Floor plan of a small office

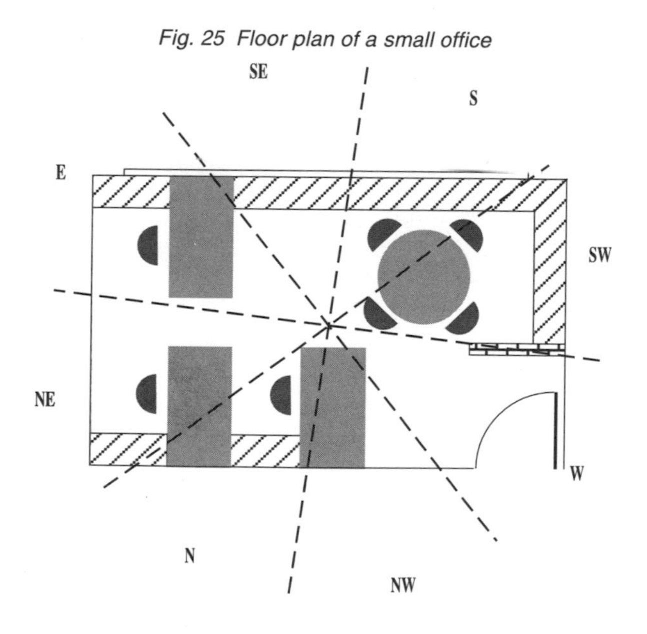

Although his entrance cannot be at the location of prosperous water stars, this drawback can be compensated for by a large window facing the prosperous water star 7. As long as the window is not blocked, the small office can still enjoy prosperity. Indeed, this young man was able to establish himself in the market a few months after going independent.

Another larger client in the textile business also selected this commercial building. He had many employees and needed to combine three units into a big office by breaking down the walls and partitions. The three units he chose were at the other end of the floor and is shown in Figure 26.

Fig. 26 Floor plan of a large office

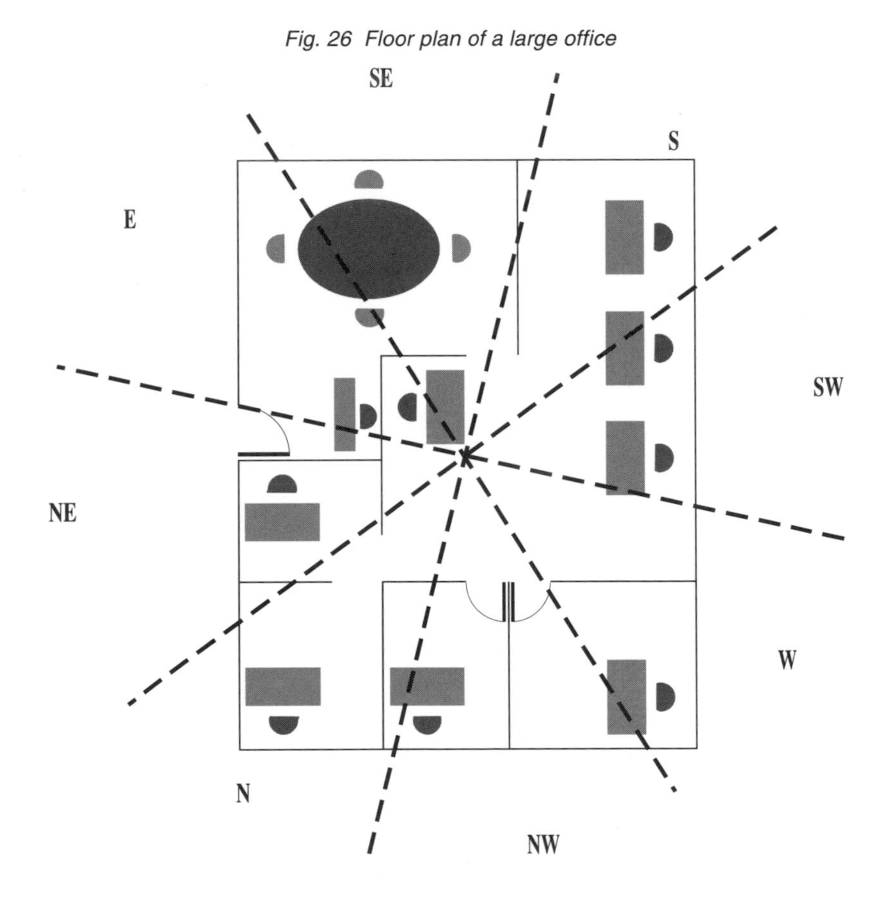

As the prosperous water star 7 is at the back of the building, I advised him to place his main entrance at the back with a spacious reception area and an open plan office to enhance the strength of the water star. As the strong mountain star 7 and 8 are both in front, all the managers' rooms were arranged in the front portion of the building.

Thus, the inherent drawback of the building, with mountain star in front and water star at the back, were remedied by a good interior arrangement. In this way, we can still convert a not too prosperous location into a prosperous office.

Where To Put Key People And Money-Making Machines

Unlike a residential flat with lots of fixed partitions, office units are often empty cubes with a great deal of flexibility for you to partition as you like. If you engage an ordinary interior designer he may help you create an impressive-looking luxurious office which, however, may not agree with *feng shui* principles. As we have seen, placing the manager's room in the location of the prosperous water star or placing the entrance in the location of the prosperous mountain star are major mistakes in *feng shui* design and can lead to grave consequences. I would, therefore, recommend that you actively participate in the interior arrangements and carefully select the location of managers' rooms, employees' tables, the reception area and generally attend to as many details as you can, following the *feng shui* principles that you have learned from this book. After you have chosen the right locations, then the interior designer can help you refine and beautify according to your own design ideas.

In designing an office, there are many items to attend to. This chapter will provide you with guidelines for every object that you place in your office.

Before you start designing your office, the following needs to be done:

1. Draw up an accurate floor plan of the office to scale.
2. Join up the diagonals of the floor plan to find the centre of the office. Then draw a circle covering the entire office.
3. Find out, as accurately as possible, the direction of each side of the office and divide the circle into eight equal sectors. Mark out the eight directions on the eight sectors.

4. Apply the *feng shui* chart of the building onto the floor plan and copy the mountain stars and water stars into each of the eight sectors.

After completing these steps, you now have a map showing the *feng shui* influences in each location of the office. With this *feng shui* map, you can exercise your creative powers and *feng shui* knowledge to work on the interior design.

Designing With Profitability In Mind

The first matter to attend to in designing an office is, of course, profitability. We have learned that profitability is governed by the prosperous water stars 7 and 8 in the *feng shui* chart and that these stars can only act if they are placed in a water location. In an office, this means that the water stars 7 and 8 must be placed in areas of activity, such as the entrance. If the entrance to the office is fortuitously located in the direction of the water star 7 or 8, I would recommend having a spacious reception area leading into the centre of the office. This way, prosperity can flow into the office without serious obstacles. If the prosperous water stars 7 or 8 are found in the direction of the window, do not block the window with partitions so that the benevolent influence can come through the window into the office.

Besides using the prosperous water stars at the entrance or windows, you may also want to design an open plan office with low partitions and low cabinets so that the circulation of prosperity will not be hampered.

Items and areas of activity, especially those closely related to marketing and incoming business, such as the fax and telex machines, can be placed at the location of the water stars 7 and 8. In some offices, the location of the prosperous stars can be reserved for the conference room or fax, telex or computer rooms. This is acceptable as they are all active functions in an office. However, I would strongly advise that only glass partitions be used in such cases so that the prosperous water stars will not be trapped within these rooms and their good influences can spill over to other parts of the office. One thing you must avoid doing is placing the water stars 7 or 8 inside a room with little activity or an enclosed room. The worst scenario is to place them inside a filing room, a store room or a toilet.

Besides the water stars 7 or 8, the location of the water star 9 is also suitable for activity, though it is not as prosperous as 7 and 8. Water star 9 is best used for conference rooms and workshops or for desks of sales representatives doing work of a more outgoing nature.

After taking care of the entrance, it is essential to select a good site for the boss's room. The boss, or the chief executive officer, is regarded as a symbol of authority and status within the office, so his office must be supported by a prosperous mountain star. The most suitable location for the room of the boss is at a sector with the prosperous mountain star 7 or 8; also, the entrance to the room should be placed in the direction of the water star 7 or 8. This configuration is called "sitting on a prosperous mountain and facing the prosperous water" and is the ideal arrangement to enhance both status and money prosperity.

Another equally important point is the external environment of the boss's office. If the office is placed in a sector of the good mountain stars, and on looking out the window, there are also tall buildings or mountains nearby in the same direction, the authority of the boss will be greater than if there is just a sea or vast open space.

After deciding on the room of the boss, you can then look at the other areas and decide how the other managers and supervisors are to be placed. Here, different businesses will have different requirements. Some require more rooms while others prefer open plan offices. For example, a lawyer's firm may need more rooms so that their lawyers can meet clients in privacy. On the other hand, a trading office with many salespeople or an engineering office with many service technicians may not even need rooms as most of the staff will often be working outdoors.

These general principles will be useful when selecting locations for your staff members:

- If the work is generally administrative in nature (for example, the work done by the accountant, the personnel manager or other administrators), the emphasis is on status and authority. These staff members are best placed in the location of the strong mountain stars 7, 8 or 9. These stars will be more effective if they are enclosed in rooms.
- If the job requires more outdoor work and the people tend to move around instead of just sit at their desks, it is best to place them in the sector with good water stars 7, 8 or 9. This arrangement is suitable for sales representatives, outdoor superintendents or engineers who are often away at the site.

So far we have only discussed the prosperous stars 7, 8 and 9. There are also many nonprosperous stars from 1 to 6. The ones to avoid are 2 and 5 as they symbolise trouble, mishap or sickness. It is therefore important not to place a key personnel in locations with the stars 2 or 5 or both. However, as mountain stars can only take effect if enclosed in a room and water stars are activated only if placed in open area, we can avoid the ill effects of 2 and 5 by enclosing the water stars 2 and 5 in a room and placing the mountain stars 2 and 5 in open space. In any case, the nonprosperous stars from 1 to 6 can still be used for less important purposes, such as the filing room, the toilet and the store room.

The theories and principles are all here. All you need is some sense of imagination to best utilise the prosperous water stars and mountain stars, subject to the physical constraints of space, the physical layout of the office and the business requirements. To help readers understand the art better, let me illustrate with an example.

An Office Layout With Good *Feng Shui*

The following floor plan shows the layout of an office in Hong Kong, designed totally according to the above *feng shui* principles. The office belongs to a large trading house listed in the Hong Kong Stock Exchange. It is located in an Age of Six building in the south-north direction. Figure 28 is the *feng shui* chart of this commercial building.

Fig. 27 Floor plan of a trading firm

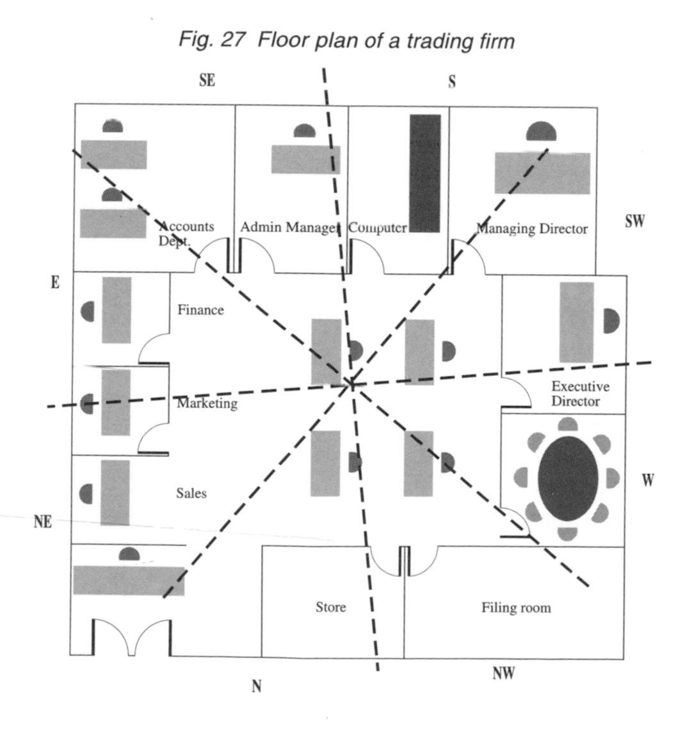

Fig. 28 Feng shui chart of a trading firm

S

9 3 5	5 7 1	7 5 3
8 4 4	1 2 6	3 9 8
4 8 9	6 6 2	2 1 7

N

The floor plan layout of this office is designed according to the locations of prosperous water stars and mountain stars. The following are the major *feng shui* features:

- The main entrance is located at the northeast. Referring to the *feng shui* chart, the prosperous water star 8 is in the northeastern square. A reception area is also located at the entrance to enhance prosperity.
- The office of the boss is located in the southwestern sector where we can find the mountain star 7. This is the ideal location, symbolising strong support and authority with the prosperous mountain star. The entrance to his room is located in the northeast, the same direction as the main entrance. The boss, thus, also enjoys the prosperity of water star 8.
- The room immediately next to the boss is the office for the deputy managing director. His office is also located in the southwestern sector to enjoy the power of the mountain star 7. Like the boss's room, his entrance also faces the northeast to receive the prosperous water star 8.
- The computer room also holds most of the essential office equipment such as faxes and telexes. This is placed in the south where the water star 7 is located. In order not to totally enclose the water star 7, glass partitions are used for this room.
- The conference room, being a room of activity, is placed in the western sector with the water star 9.
- The other strong mountain stars of 8 and 9 are placed in the southeastern and eastern sectors. These sectors are suitable for administrators such as the personnel manager, the chief accountant and the marketing manager. Four rooms are located in these two sectors.

- Another partition is located near the entrance in the northeast. This area is under the influence of the water star 8 which is best used for the sales representatives.
- The central main hall is left for open plan office. The marketing people are placed in sectors within the northeast, the south and the west to enjoy the water stars 8, 7 and 9. The other sectors are less prosperous and will be occupied by clerical staff whose jobs are less vital to profit making.
- The northwestern and the northern sectors are dominated by the nonprosperous stars of 2, 1 and 6. These areas are best used as filing rooms and rooms for employees whose jobs are not related to sales.

This example illustrates how we can design the location of various functional departments within an office. However, the task is not finished yet. In the next chapter, we will take a look at the more detailed interior decorations of an office.

Interior Design For Maximum Profits

Some Western writers define *feng shui* as the art of placement of objects. This is one of the better definitions as *feng shui* deals mainly with the theories of how we can place various items in the universe so as to exploit the benefit of the forces of nature and to achieve harmony. The evaluation of *feng shui* for houses actually deals with the placement of people into the best environment. Yin house *feng shui*—the technique of burying ancestors in well chosen grave sites—is, in fact, the art of placing the body in the best location to receive the benevolent influence of nature. *Feng shui* can thus be viewed as a wisdom revealing how to place objects. Such theories can be applied in real life in our placement of furniture and decorations.

After deciding on the location of each room and functional department within an office, we now come to the interesting part of how to place our furniture and decorate the office to exploit the best *feng shui* influences.

Designing the floor plan layout is only the first step. It assigns the right location for each person and each function within an office. However, this is far from completes the *feng shui* design. We still require correct placement of furniture inside the office and within each room to ensure that the good locations are properly utilised and the bad and nonprosperous stars are avoided.

The *feng shui* chart of a building shows all the directional influences in relation to a point or an object. There is no space limitation to its usage. As we have seen, the *feng shui* chart is obtained from the direction of the building. So any object, whether large or small, is also subject to the influence of the same *feng shui* chart as long as it is inside the building. In the last chapter, the chart was applied to the office unit inside the building. Likewise, it can also be applied to any small section or sub-unit within the office unit. We can apply the same chart inside a single room to see the influences in different locations of the room, or even apply the same chart to our desktop to see the *feng shui* influence in the different corners of our desk. Hence, the chart of the building is still the fundamental reference for us to design the placement of furniture and objects within our office.

After selecting the location for each room, the next major task is to determine where to place the desk and entrance for each room. These two items must be considered together as they are interrelated. When designing the interior of a room, you need to take the same steps as if you were designing the layout of the entire office described in the last chapter. The first step is to draw a simple sketch of the room, find its centre, use the centre to draw a circle, and then find out the eight directions and divide the circle into eight equal sectors. Then look at the *feng shui* chart of the building and copy the mountain stars and water stars to each sector of the circle. Through this method, you can see clearly what *feng shui* influence each sector of your room receives. This provides the guidance for decorating the room.

Before designing the interior decorations, it is necessary to set the location of the entrance first. As the entrance to the individual office is also a location of activity, it is too governed by the water stars. Therefore, it is best to place the entrance to a room at the location of one of the prosperous water stars 7, 8 or 9. The bad water stars of 5 and 2 should be avoided by all means. The best entrance to the boss's room is not only located at the direction of the prosperous water stars, as viewed from the centre of his room, but also located in same direction as the main entrance to the office, if the main entrance is placed in the sector of the best water stars.

Another point to note is that the entrance to each individual office should not be placed at the corners of the main hall. It is believed that the *feng shui* influences entering the main door will reach the corners first, where they gather before bouncing and circulating to the entire floor. The corners are thus similar to the bottom of a bottle used to hold the *feng shui* forces. Because of this, solid walls are needed at the corners for the *feng shui* to bounce back and circulate. An entrance at these corners is like a leak at the bottom of a bottle—the *feng shui* influences will leak out without circulating throughout the entire office.

Fig. 29 Leakage of benevolent feng shui influence

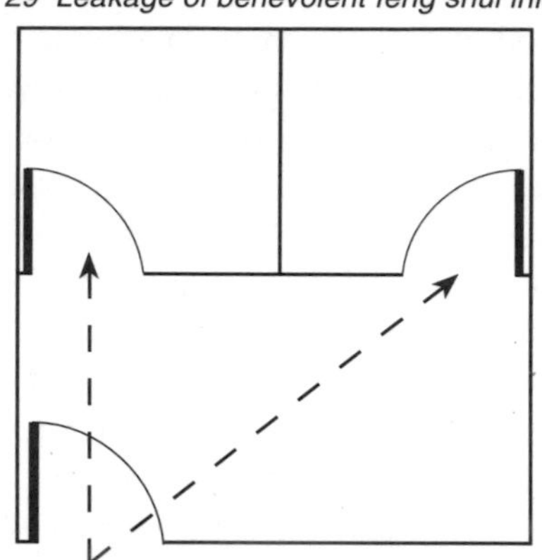

Some Guidelines For Placement of Desks

After determining the entrance to the office rooms, let us now see how we should place the desks inside each room or partition. The following are some guidelines:

- The prosperous mountain stars of 7, 8 or 9 are symbols of power and authority. For a manager or supervisor to sit authoritatively, it is necessary to place the desk within the sector where the prosperous mountain stars are located.
- The natural position for placing the desk should be at the corner of the diagonal line from the entrance, so that the person can face and see the entrance at an angle. Sitting on a straight line towards the entrance, or with your back against the entrance, is not recommended.

Fig. 30 Proper desk arrangement

Fig. 31 Bad desk arrangements

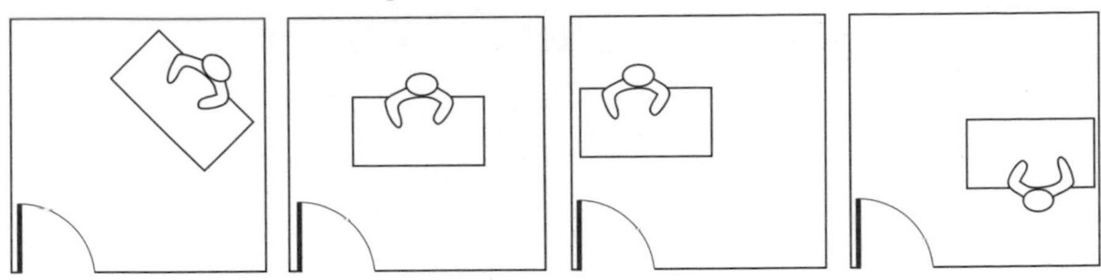

- To enhance the symbol of authority, the desk should lean against a solid wall. Similarly, the person should sit with his back against a solid wall. I would advise against placing the desk in the middle of the room without leaning against any wall. It gives the impression of floating on air and insecurity. I would also not recommend placing the desk at the corner without leaning against any wall (Figure 31).
- The desk should not be placed at the location of the bad mountain stars 5 or 2.

As the office desk is where a manager sits for much of his working day and is very important to his personal well being and the prosperity of the business, it is best to follow all the rules laid down above. In practice, however, satisfying all the criteria is difficult and some sacrifices and compromises may have to be made.

We have discussed how to place desks inside office rooms. For desks in open plan offices, the same general principles can be applied. As a guideline, employees whose major job responsibilities include administration should be placed in sectors with strong mountain stars. Employees whose jobs require more creativity will be better placed in sectors of prosperous water stars with as few partitions as possible.

Besides attending to the location of desks, one should also ensure that the table arrangement outside will not cause a "shar" or bad *feng shui* influence for managers sitting inside the rooms. Desk arrangements which form sharp angles or a long line forming a rectangular block shape with one end pointing at the manager are not desirable.

Fig. 32 Shars created by other desks

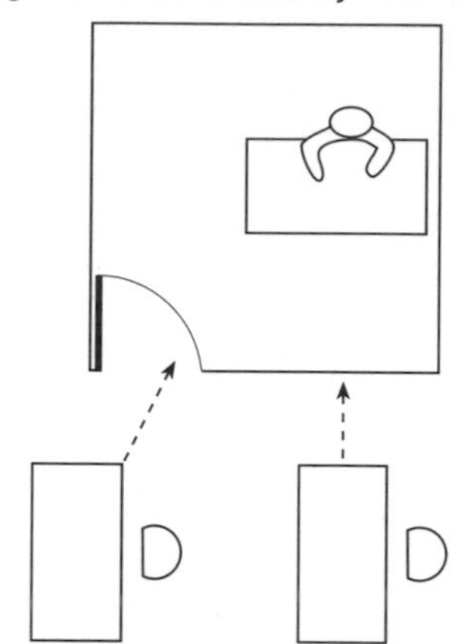

Besides the placement of desks, there are many other small items to attend to in office decoration. It is difficult to explain each item one by one. However, as every item can be classified as either active or inactive, we can generalise by the principle that active items should be placed in the location of the prosperous water stars and inactive items are best placed in the location of prosperous mountain stars. For example, the telephone, the fax machine and the computer are active items. The bookshelf and cabinet are inactive items. Active items like the telephone should be placed in the direction or location of prosperous water stars 7 or 8. If your telephone is placed on a desk top, you can place it in a prosperous water star sector of your desk top, if you divide your desk into eight sectors in same manner as your room.

After arranging the desks, cabinets and office equipment, our task is still incomplete as we need to attend to other decorative problems such as the colour scheme and decorative objects such as plants, flowers and fish tanks. These arrangements require the technique of the Four Pillars of Destiny and will be discussed in the next chapter.

Interior Design For A Restaurant

So far I have introduced to readers the *feng shui* technique of placement and decoration for an office. The same principles of the flying stars can be applied to all types of business environments, including shops and restaurants. The following diagram shows the interior layout of a restaurant located at the Victoria Peak. The corresponding *feng shui* chart is also shown in Figure 33.

Fig. 33 Interior layout of a restaurant and its feng shui chart

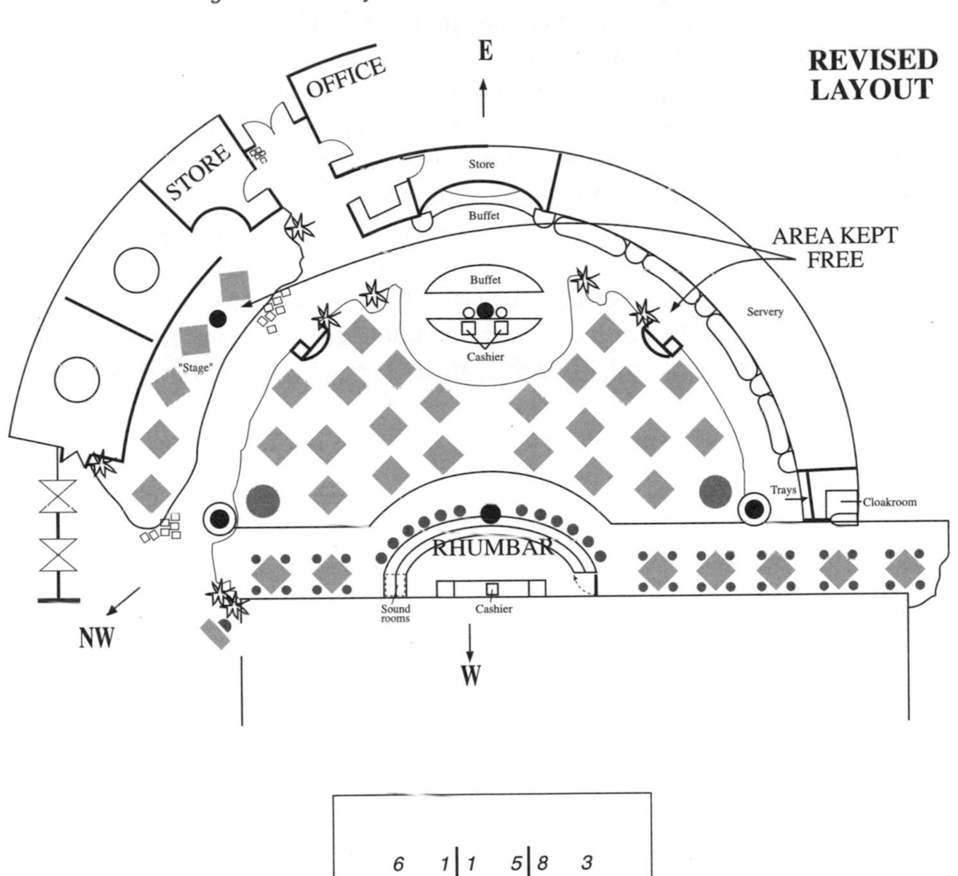

E				W
	6 1 **6**	1 5 **2**	8 3 **4**	
E	7 2 **5**	5 9 **7**	3 7 **9**	W
	2 6 **1**	9 4 **3**	4 8 **8**	

This is an Age of Seven building and the semicircle-shaped restaurant sits with its back against the east and its front facing west. The essential items in the interior design for such a restaurant are the entrances, the cashier's counter, the office and places of activity such as the dance floor, bandstand, kitchen and tables. The *feng shui* chart indicates that the prosperous water star 7 is in the front (west) and the mountain star 7 is at the back (east). Another pair of prosperous stars 8 are located in the northwest and the southwest. If readers compare the chart against the floor layout, it is easy to see that the arrangement closely follows the rule that the active areas be placed in the location of the prosperous water star. The main entrance and the band stand are located in the northwest with the water star 8. The cashier's counter is located in the east with its back against the mountain star 7 and its front facing the water star 7.

ADOPTING THE RIGHT COLOUR AND LOGO

An interior designer advises his client on the basis of comfort, taste, budget and nature of business. These are valid factors to consider when decorating an office. But there is still something missing because a comfortable and luxuriously decorated office does not automatically bring profitability. For a business to prosper, we require a profitable *feng shui* environment with the right interior arrangements and decorations. We have already discussed how to go about placing the entrances, rooms, desks and office equipment in the right locations. In this chapter we are going to complete the task of achieving a prosperous *feng shui* environment by selecting the right colour and objects for decoration.

I always remind my students that the subject of *feng shui* and the Four Pillars of Destiny are interrelated and that one can never be a good *feng shui* expert without mastering the technique of the Four Pillars of Destiny. Indeed, the technique of the Four Pillars of Destiny needs to be applied in decorating our business environment. One example is the choice of colours.

The technique of the Four Pillars of Destiny has been discussed in the first section of this book. To refresh the reader's memory, our destiny is a mixture of the five basic elements—metal, wood, water, fire and earth. These five elements not only symbolise the five basic forces in the universe but are also the basic components of human destiny. The five elements are interlinked by the Cycle of Birth and the Cycle of Destruction, so our fortunes are continuously subject to the interactions of the five elements.

In general, a good balance of strength among the basic elements in our destiny will bring harmony. On the other hand, an imbalance brought about by the excessive presence of some elements can cause misfortune. From a set of four pillars, we can identify some elements which will enhance harmony. By the same token, we can also identify some elements which will bring about imbalance and cause misfortune. We call the former favourable elements and the later, unfavourable elements. These elements often come in pairs of more than two but seldom exceed three in number. The reason is that the most favourable element also needs support from another element. So the element that supports the most favourable element becomes the second best. The same can be said of unfavourable elements.

Take, for example, a person born in winter, whose day pillar is fire. This is a weak fire which needs wood to provide nourishment. Obviously, wood is the most favourable element. Water generates wood. Hence water becomes second best. Other fire means colleagues and friends who will support him. So fire is not bad. The remaining two elements—earth and metal—are unfavourable. Metal is the worst as it destroys wood to cut off the supply of nourishment to the fire. Earth is the second worst as earth generates more metal and destroys water.

The five elements are, in fact, symbols of everything in our universe. If you know what your favourable elements are, you should, by all means, enhance the influence of these elements by putting yourself in an environment with plenty of these elements. This is because the favourable elements will bring personal prosperity and harmony to your life. One direct elemental influence comes from the cosmos. We have daily, monthly and yearly influences as reflected by the heavenly stems and earthly branches found in the Chinese calendar. However, these elemental influences are abstract, seasonal and totally beyond our control. Bad luck will come if the unfavourable elements feature prominently in a certain period or year. However, the positive side is that all the physical objects in the universe can also be classified into the five elements. We can thus control the elemental influences in our physical surroundings just by choosing the right physical objects and avoiding the bad objects. This is how we can enhance our prosperity by *feng shui* decorations according to the elements we require in our destiny.

The most impressive decoration in an office or residence is the colour scheme, so we should place ourselves in a colour scheme belonging to our favourable elements.

The following list shows how each colour is related to an element:

Metal — white, silver, gold, metallic
Wood — green, blue, brown.
Water — black, grey
Fire — red, purple, pink
Earth — yellow, beige

In the above example, the man is a weak fire person who needs the wood element. The best colour tone for his office is green, blue or brown. He should avoid white, gold, silver and yellow as they are symbols of metal and earth which are elements not favourable to him. Thus, if he is the boss of the office, he should paint the walls, lay his carpets or use furniture in colour tones of green, blue or brown. He has the option to choose light or dark colours according to his personal taste but normally, dark colours are more suited for the home or for rooms which need more privacy.

Besides symbolising colours, the five elements can also be found in all decorative objects. The corresponding elements for some common decorative or furniture items are listed below:

Metal — metallic objects, round objects, silvery or golden objects.
Wood — plants, wooden furniture, long and rectangular objects.
Water — fish tanks, pools.
Fire — sharp pointed objects, red coloured posters or pictures, red lights, red carpets, cooking stove.
Earth — pottery and porcelain, clay and mud, square-shaped blocks.

One can then select from the table the suitable decorative objects according to one's favourable elements. The weak fire man illustrated in the above example should use more plants to decorate his room and should avoid placing too many metallic objects or pottery in his surrounding environment.

Choosing The Right Logo

When starting a new business, an important concern is finding a suitable logo. The logo is the symbol of the business and the Chinese often attach great significance to such symbolism. A good logo should not only be artistic and attractive, it should also reflect the nature of the business. Furthermore, it should shoulder the task of enhancing the prosperity of the business as well. Therefore, designing a suitable and prosperous logo is very important.

When designing the logo, one has to chose both the object and colour to represent the business. This is very similar to selecting suitable decorative objects and colour schemes to decorate the office, and the same principle of choosing the favourable elements can be applied. For example, if the man of weak fire is the head of the company, the most suitable logo for him is a flower or a plant in green and brown, as all these are related to the wood element which will bring him harmony and personal prosperity.

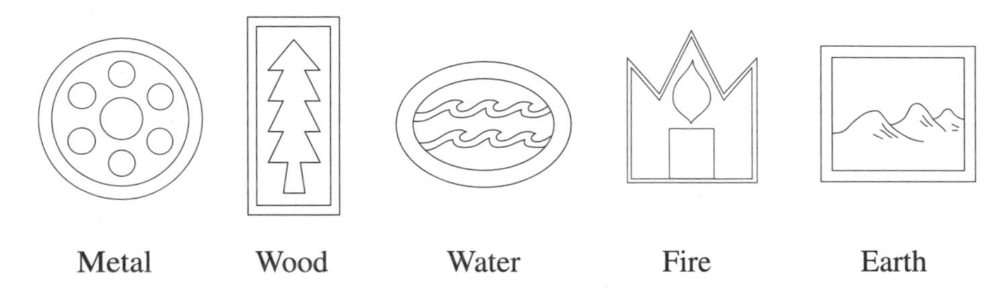

Fig. 34 Some sample logos symbolising elements

Colour Advice For Elton John

For a deeper understanding of this technique, let us examine a real set of Four Pillars of Destiny and use it as an exercise to study the suitable colour and decorative objects.

The Pillars of Destiny of Elton John

Hour	Day	Month	Year
?	癸 Water	癸 Water	丁 Fire
?	卯 Wood	卯 Wood	亥 Water

56	46	36	26	16	6
丁 Fire	戊 Earth	己 Earth	庚 Metal	辛 Metal	壬 Water
酉 Metal	戌 Earth	亥 Water	子 Water	丑 Earth	寅 Wood

The above three pillars belong to British rock superstar Mr. Elton John. His birth data, translated into pillars of destiny, shows that he is a water

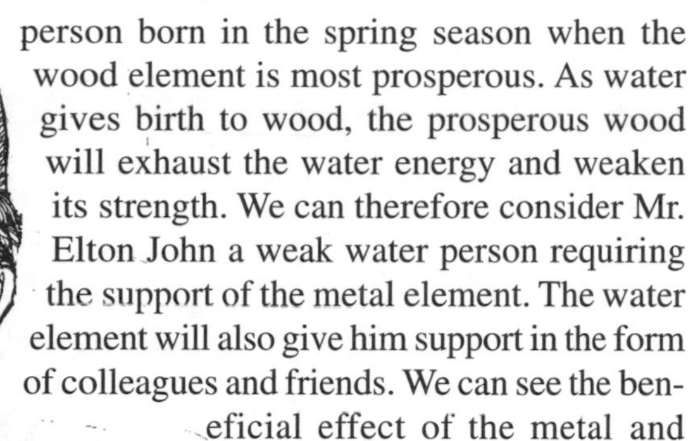

person born in the spring season when the wood element is most prosperous. As water gives birth to wood, the prosperous wood will exhaust the water energy and weaken its strength. We can therefore consider Mr. Elton John a weak water person requiring the support of the metal element. The water element will also give him support in the form of colleagues and friends. We can see the beneficial effect of the metal and water elements by tracing the past successes of Mr. John. Mr. John was under the most favourable influence of metal and water in the luck pillar between the age of 26 and 36. He achieved mammoth successes in his concert and record sales during this period in the 1970s. His musical career reached its peak in the years between 1973 and the late seventies. Ardent Elton John fans will recall that his most successful double LP *Goodbye Yellow Brick Road* was released in 1973 when he was about 26 years old and entering his best luck pillar of metal and water.

If Mr. John decides to decorate his office and engages you as a *feng shui* expert, you can recommend that he use the colour tones of white or metallic, symbolising metal, and some black or grey furniture, symbolising water. A little yellow is also acceptable as it symbolises the earth element which gives support to metal. His best decorative objects should be golden or metallic articles; he can even place a fish tank with gold fish in a prosperous location in his office. On the other hand, wood and fire elements are not too favourable to him as they will exhaust the water energy. He should use less red, purple and green colours and not place too many plants in his room. You can also advise him to wear more black and white or metallic coloured clothes which will bring him greater success.

Feng Shui Maintenance And Trouble-Shooting

If you have chosen a good *feng shui* location for your office and have done the interior arrangements and decorations according to *feng shui* rules, you have already laid down the foundation for prosperity in your business. However, *feng shui* attention to your environment is not an one-off job. Good *feng shui* design is fundamental to the inherent harmony and prosperity of the environment but it does not make the environment totally immune to misfortune.

As the universe is everchanging, *feng shui* influences will also change continuously with time. Many Chinese emperors were firm *feng shui* believers and engaged the top *feng shui* experts in the country to design their palaces and tombs. Despite all this, dynasties continued to rise and fall in Chinese history and no royal family has managed to last forever. The reason is that *feng shui* changes in cycles and we need continuous attention to maintain the prosperous influences and to avoid bad influences. Any carelessness in adjusting ourselves to the changes may bring misfortune. The intensity of such misfortunes is subject to the original *feng shui* design of the environment. Thus we must not discount the process of carefully choosing a good *feng shui* location and devising a good *feng shui* design. If the original design is good, should some bad *feng shui* influences arrive, the intensity of misfortune is reduced. On the other hand, if the original *feng shui* design is not up to standard, then any bad *feng shui* influence will be intensified to create huge misfortunes or losses.

The *feng shui* intangible forces, or the flying stars, change continuously with time according to a fixed pattern of the Lo Shu diagram as introduced in earlier chapters. So it is possible for us to foresee which star will arrive at what location at a certain period of time. In theory, we can predict the *feng shui* influence from day to day, even from hour to hour. But this is too tedious; the common practice is to make major adjustments yearly and minor adjustments monthly. To make correct adjustments, we have to attend to both the yearly and monthly flying stars.

The yearly flying stars change from the first day of the spring season, which usually falls on 4 or 5 February of the Western calendar, and last for a year until the next 4 or 5 February. The basic change is in the middle number of the nine squares, which is the controlling number of the year. Once the middle number is changed, the other numbers in the surrounding eight squares change correspondingly in the same pattern of the original Lo Shu diagram. The direction of movement is centre - NW - W - NE - S - N - SW - E - SE. Once we know the centre number, we can immediately derive the other numbers in the eight surrounding squares. For example, 6 is the controlling number going into the middle in the year 1996. We can then draw up the nine square chart for the year 1996 as follows:

Fig. 35 Flying star chart for 1996

	clash star 3 shars	
3	8	1
2	4	6
7	9	5
	year star	

The above is the flying star *feng shui* chart for the year 1996. It shows us the *feng shui* influences prevailing in all directions in 1996. For example, the bad star 5 is in the northwestern square. If your room or entrance is located in the northwest, it means that they will come under bad influence in 1996, making it necessary to take some precautions. The bad star 5 is of the earth category and earth will give birth to metal according to the cycle of birth. A metal object will help exhaust the power of the 5 and dissolve its bad effects. So the common practice is to hang a metal windchime on the ceiling of the northwestern room, or inside the entrance of the northwestern door. The metal windchime will generate metallic noise which will reduce the bad earth energy.

Another bad influence to note is the number 2 which arrives in the eastern square according to the *feng shui* chart of 1996. This number means sickness and the common way to dissolve it is to hang a string of six metal coins in the affected location in the east.

The number 3, found in the southeastern square, is also not a good star and will bring agitation and anger. As 3 belongs to the wood category, the way to dissolve it is to place red objects, such as a red poster or carpet, in the affected location. Red is the colour of fire so it is able to dissolve the unfavourable wood power of the 3.

The numbers 1, 4 and 6 are not favourable numbers in the present Age of Seven but they will not bring serious mishaps. However, 6 also related to law and litigation so it may bring legal entanglements which are not desirable. The way to dissolve the 6 is to place water, black objects or plants. The 6 is in the west in 1996.

The prosperous numbers are 8 and 7 which are in the south and northeast of the chart in 1996. These are stars that will bring better fortune. If your main entrance is located at the northeast or south and the original *feng shui* chart of the building shows the water star 7 in these locations, you can predict a very prosperous year in 1996. This is because the 8 in the earth category will enhance the good effect of the water star 7 which is a metal element.

Besides all these stars, there are also some influences which are not normally shown in the flying star chart. The first is the "year star" which, in the past, was related to the direction of the planet Jupiter in a certain year. In 1996, it is in the north. You can sit on the "year star" but should not face and challenge it. So sitting in the exact south, facing north, is not recommended in 1996. The south is directly opposite the year star and is called the "clash star" location. It is inadvisable to disturb the location of the year star. Thus you should not carry out large scale construction work in the north in the year of the Rat (1996).

Another location to note is the "seat of three shars" which is the direction in which its elements clash and are in a destructive relationship with the "year star". In 1996, the "seat of three shars" is, like the "clash star", located in the south. Sitting in the exact south therefore attracts trouble and obstacles. I would recommend you change your sitting position if you happen to sit with your back against exact south in 1996.

The above example is based on the year 1996. In Appendix 8 of this book, I have listed out the locations of the flying stars, year stars, clash stars and three shars from 1992 until 2009. Readers can check the locations and take yearly precautions according to the above guidance.

So far I have shown you examples of how we should perform *feng shui* maintenance work year by year. However, there are also *feng shui* charts for each of the 12 months in a year. The operation of the monthly flying star charts is same as that of the yearly charts. A controlling number goes to the centre and the other numbers are distributed in the same manner as the Lo Shu diagram. The monthly star often tells us the timing of misfortunes. For example, the year star 5 is in the east in 1993. The east is generally not good for that year but things get worse when the month star 5 or the other bad star 2 arrives in the east. The monthly controlling star 4 moved to the centre in June 1993, bringing the bad star 2 to the east to join forces with the bad year star 5 already present in the east. We can thus anticipate that June 1993 is a time to take special care if one happens to stay in an east room or a room facing an east entrance.

Up to now we have only emphasized the nature of yearly stars and monthly stars without referring to the original *feng shui* chart of the office building itself. In practice, the original *feng shui* chart of the environment plays an important role in determining whether a yearly or monthly bad star will bring mishap. If you have placed yourself in a room with the very prosperous mountain star 7 or 8 and you have opened your entrances in the locations of the water stars 7 or 8, even the arrival of the yearly bad stars 5 or 2 will not bring serious trouble.

One can analyse the actual effect of a year star on the *feng shui* of an office by comparing the yearly chart against the office building *feng shui* chart. The general principle is that if a prosperous water star 7 or 8 is placed in the right location according to the rule of placing a prosperous water star in water and a prosperous mountain star on the mountain, the arrival of a star that destroys or gives birth to the 7 or 8 will enhance the prosperity. The arrival of a star that will be given birth to or destroyed by the 7 or 8 will reduce the prosperity. This sounds very complicated but is not too difficult to understand if illustrated by an example.

If your entrance is located at the place of water star 7, like the example of the Hongkong Bank's north entrance, in the year 1993, the year star 3 arrives in the north. Since the 3 is wood and the 7 is metal, the 7 will destroy 3 and exhaust its energy. So we cannot expect 1993 to be a very prosperous year for the Hongkong Bank as the power of the prosperous water star 7 is dissipated by it spending its energy to destroy the year star 3.

Ill Effects From The Bank Of China Building

Let me illustrate with another interesting example. A recent *feng shui* controversy in Hong Kong is the apparent ill effect of the new Bank of China building on the Governor's House. The Bank of China building is a very tall building and its upper parts are triangular shapes that create large sharp edges. One of these sharp edge points towards the back of the Governor's House. Since the erection of the new Bank of China building in the east of the Governor's House, there have been several mishaps. The Governor Sir Edward Youde died of a heart attack while on a business trip to Beijing in 1986, and his successor, Sir David Wilson, also suffered injuries during a morning exercise walk. The present Governor Chris Patten suffered heart trouble shortly after his arrival in Hong Kong in 1992; sickness also struck his family members.

A huge building with special shapes will certainly cast *feng shui* influence on nearby buildings. But how do we assess its influence and make predictions? To assess the effect of the Bank of China building on the Governor's House, the first step is to examine the *feng shui* chart of the Governor's House and see what are the stars in the location of the Bank of China building. Figure 37 shows the *feng shui* chart of the Governor's House.

Fig. 36 Sketch of the environment of the Governor's House

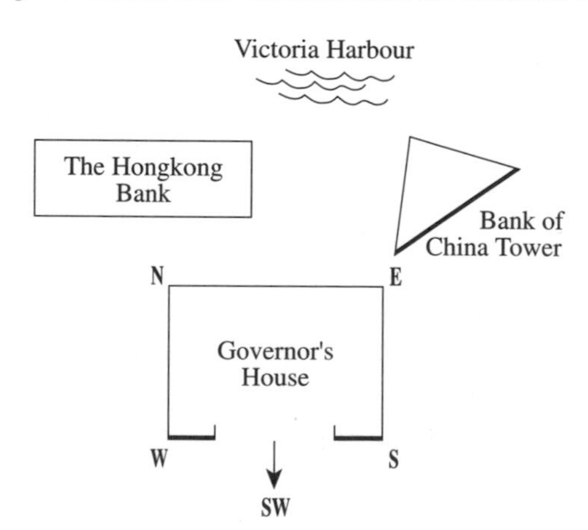

Fig. 37 Feng shui chart of the Governor's House

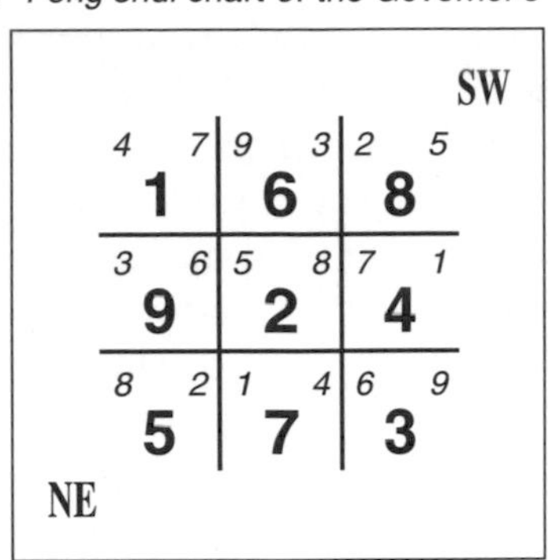

The Bank of China building is located to the east of the Governor's House. As it is a tall building, it enhances the effect of the mountain star in the eastern square. From the chart we can see the mountain star is 3. Now, the star 3 is a bad star symbolising agitation and anger. Therefore, it is logical to predict that there will be less human harmony but more conflict. The star number 3 is also a symbol of robbery and crime. As a matter of fact, crime has been on the rise in Hong Kong since 1990. Crime and conflict was most serious in 1992 with robberies involving the use of heavy arms such as AK-47 machine guns. Conflict also emerged between the British and Chinese governments over political reform issues in Hong Kong and the financial arrangement for the new Hong Kong airport. Such conflicts are also reflected in the flying star charts of the Governor's House.

In 1992, when the yearly controlling star is 8, the year star 6 arrives in the east. The original mountain star in the east is 3 which is a bad star of the wood element while the metal star 6 is a destroyer of wood. This does not result in suppression of the 3, but, in fact, stimulates its bad effects. So 1992 was a year of very serious robberies in Hong Kong.

Now let us look at 1993. In articles released to the media in Hong Kong at the beginning of 1993, I predicted that law and order in Hong Kong would improve and that there would be fewer robberies than in 1992. This prediction was made on the grounds that in 1993, the year star 5 moves to the east. The 5 is of earth category and will be destroyed by the 3 which is wood. The 3, by destroying the 5, exhausts its own energy and so its ill effect is reduced. This prediction proved accurate and no further serious robberies with heavy arms occurred in Hong Kong in 1993.

In 1994, the year star 6 moved to the centre while the year star 4 arrived in the east. Now, 4 belongs to the wood element. When it encountered the 3 in the eastern sector of the Governor's House, it became a case of wood reinforcing wood. So the crime rate could be expected to worsen compared to 1993. However, the nature of the crimes was not similar to 1992. Instead of armed robberies, Hong Kong saw a wave of sex crimes in 1994. In fact, one sex criminal was sentenced to life imprisonment several times over for raping and killing many victims. What happened can be easily explained if readers refer back to the table on page 75. The year star 4, after all, carries the meaning of sex and romance!

In this chapter, I have demonstrated that there are many ways to manipulate the *feng shui* numbers and that the numbers can help us make predictions with startling accuracy. The process appears complicated at first glance, but if you go through the examples again, you will notice that all the predictions are based on the simple relationships of birth and destruction among the five basic elements. Once you have memorised these simple relationships by heart, then the key is to use your logical mind to make deductions from these rules. Your skill and confidence will improve considerably with practice and in time, you will find it possible to peep into the future and become master of your own destiny.

AUSPICIOUS DATES FOR BUSINESS

A common custom of the Chinese is to select an auspicious date for important events. It is believed that choosing a good date not only ensures that the event has a smooth and prosperous beginning, but also enhances its chances of future success and prosperity. Many Chinese will carefully select a suitable date for events such as the opening ceremony of a business venture, a marriage ceremony or the day for moving into new premises.

Years ago, almost every Chinese family owned a book called the *Tung Shing* (or *Tung Shu*, meaning the handy book). This book is a Chinese almanac advising all the suitable activities day by day in a year. Activities ranged from important events like marriage and opening ceremonies to trivial matters like moving furniture and washing one's hair. The *Tung Shing* was considered an essential guide for Chinese household affairs and everyone would check the almanac to ensure that all occasions were held on an auspicious date.

Despite the onslaught of Western influences, this custom is still very much alive today. The *Tung Shing* continues to sell millions of copies every year with Chinese throughout the world consulting the almanac for important events. I would not recommend consulting the *Tung Shing* for trivial matters such as the best time to wash your hair. However, this book does embrace the wisdom of both *feng shui* and the Four Pillars of Destiny and is a handy reference book for any businessman who wishes to choose an auspicious date for the opening ceremony of his office or shop.

How important is the opening ceremony? The success or failure of a business concern or a marriage depends on many factors. If a business or marriage goes wrong afterwards, we can always attribute the failure to the bad *feng shui* of the office or residence as well as misfortune or incompatibility reflected in the Four Pillars of Destiny. So it is impossible to verify whether a badly chosen commencement date is an attribute. However, traditionally, the Chinese regard the commencement date of any event as as important as the birthday of a child. Even in Western astrology, there is a branch called mundane astrology which casts horoscopes of an organisation according to the date of birth (which is the commencement date of the organisation). Using such a horoscope, the astrologer is able to chart the course of the organisation. In Chinese metaphysics, the art of selecting a date involves very complicated knowledge of several subjects, including astronomy, *feng shui* and the Four Pillars of Destiny.

The selection of an auspicious date carries such significance that it is regarded as a separate and highly specialised subject in Chinese metaphysics. It will be too ambitious to explain the art in detail in this book. However, I believe it is necessary to provide readers with some basic ideas.

When introducing the technique of date selection, a major drawback is that the *Tung Shing* is generally not available in English. Even if it was, the auspicious dates marked in the almanac would not be suitable for everyone as it is an over-generalised book that does not take into consideration the uniqueness of individual destinies. Therefore, it is still necessary to learn ways to select a good date without relying on the *Tung Shing*. The purpose of this chapter is to introduce some criteria for readers to select a good date for their important events like the opening ceremony of a new business.

As introduced in the first few chapters of this book, the Chinese calendar system is basically a calendar which reflects the influence of the five basic elements at a certain point of time. The purpose of selecting an auspicious date is to ensure one gets the best influence of the basic elements on the date of the important event as well as over the long term. To ensure that the date we perform the event is harmonious, we need to fully understand the interrelationships among the five elements. In the section about the Four Pillars of Destiny, I have already introduced the cycle of destruction and the cycle of birth among the five elements. Now let us examine another type of relationship—clash and combine relations.

In the Chinese calendar, there are a total of 22 Chinese characters. Ten are called heavenly stems while the other 12 are called earthly branches. The earthly branches are related to one another by clash or combine relationships. As the terms suggest, clash means conflict and confrontation while combine means harmony and peace. The following table shows pairs of earthly branches which are in clash and combine positions:

Earthly Branches in Clash Positions

子 Yang Water (Rat)	—	午 Yang Fire (Horse)
丑 Yin Earth (Ox)	—	未 Yin Earth (Goat)
寅 Yang Wood (Tiger)	—	申 Yang Metal (Monkey)
卯 Yin Wood (Rabbit)	—	酉 Yin Metal (Rooster)
辰 Yang Earth (Dragon)	—	戌 Yang Earth (Dog)
巳 Yin Fire (Snake)	—	亥 Yin Water (Pig)

Earthly Branches in Combine Positions

子 Yang Water (Rat)	—	丑 Yin Earth (Ox)
寅 Yang Wood (Tiger)	—	亥 Yin Water (Pig)
卯 Yin Wood (Rabbit)	—	戌 Yang Earth (Dog)
辰 Yang Earth (Dragon)	—	酉 Yin Metal (Rooster)
巳 Yin Fire (Snake)	—	申 Yang Metal (Monkey)
午 Yang Fire (Horse)	—	未 Yin Earth (Goat)

Readers can see that clash relations always occur in elements in destructive relationships, such as wood clashing against metal or water clashing against fire, the exception being earth clashing against itself.

As clash means conflict, the first rule in date selecting is not to use days when the earthly branch is in a clash position against the earthly branch of the month. For example, if an event is scheduled to take place on the second month of the Chinese year, the earthly branch of such a month will be " 卯 ", meaning yin wood. If you conduct an opening ceremony in such a month, you need to avoid the day when the earthly branch is yin metal as yin metal is in a clash position against yin wood. Such a date of yin wood in a month of yin metal is called a "clash date" and is generally regarded as a bad date for conducting important events. By the same token, when choosing the hour to begin the ceremony on a certain day, you should avoid the "clash hour". For example, in a date of yin wood, the clash hour is yin metal, which is the hour between 5 and 7 p.m.

For the same reason of avoiding conflict and confrontations, try to avoid choosing a day which is in a clash configuration against the birth year of the person or persons involved. For example, if you are the head of a business venture selecting a day to conduct the opening ceremony for your shop or office, you need to know your own Four Pillars of Destiny first. From your Four Pillars of Destiny, you can find out the element of your birth year. The emphasis is on the earthly branches. For instance, if you are born in the year 1951, which is a year of yin wood in the earthly branch, you should avoid selecting a day with yin metal as the earthly branch for conducting the ceremony. A date of yin metal is in a clash position against your birth year—yin wood. So the date is regarded as a bad date, bringing conflict and disharmony to the person.

In Chinese metaphysics, the clash relationship among earthly branches is considered taboo and must be avoided at all costs. The earthly branch of a day may clash against the year, the month or the birth year of the person. It may also clash against the back of the building or the back of the manager's seat. In *feng shui*, the earthly branches symbolise directions. If your building or your seat faces west with its back against the east, I would advise against choosing a date of yin metal. The reason is that yin metal symbolises the west and yin wood symbolises the east. A day of yin metal will therefore clash against the east direction—the yin wood—which is the back of the building or the back of your seat.

So far I have listed out several taboos to be avoided when selecting a good date. Now I will provide some guidelines for what you should do. If the opening ceremony runs into trouble or misfortune happens during such an event, the Chinese consider this a bad omen symbolising future obstacles in the business venture. Hence, it is important to ensure that everything goes smoothly on that day. To do so, it is best that the day be chosen according to the favourable element of the boss. Examine the pillars of destiny of the boss to find out his favourable elements. If he is a weak wood person requiring water as nourishment, then a day with strong water element should be chosen.

Auspicious Dates For Michael Jackson

Let me illustrate with a simple example. The following pillars of destiny belongs to the dynamic entertainer Mr. Michael Jackson.

The Pillars of Destiny of Michael Jackson (29/8/1958)

Hour	Day	Month	Year
?	戊 Earth	庚 Metal	戊 Earth
?	寅 Wood	申 Metal	戌 Earth

He is an earth person born in autumn with very strong metal elements in his month pillar. Since metal is generated by earth, metal is the symbol of creativity and intelligence of an earth person. The prominent presence of the metal element in Mr. Jackson's destiny reflects his talent as a great performer and singer. However, metal will exhaust earth energy. The strong presence of metal reflects weak earth, and Mr. Jackson requires the support of fire and wood. These are his favourable elements. On the other hand, metal and water will exhaust earth energy and are therefore unfavourable elements.

Using this hypothesis, if Mr. Jackson needs to select a date for starting a new business venture or signing a new recording contract, he should select a day with a strong presence of fire and wood as these elements will enhance his fortune and harmony. A day of strong metal or water should be avoided. As he was born in the year of the dog, a day of the dragon should also be avoided as the dragon is in a clash position against the dog.

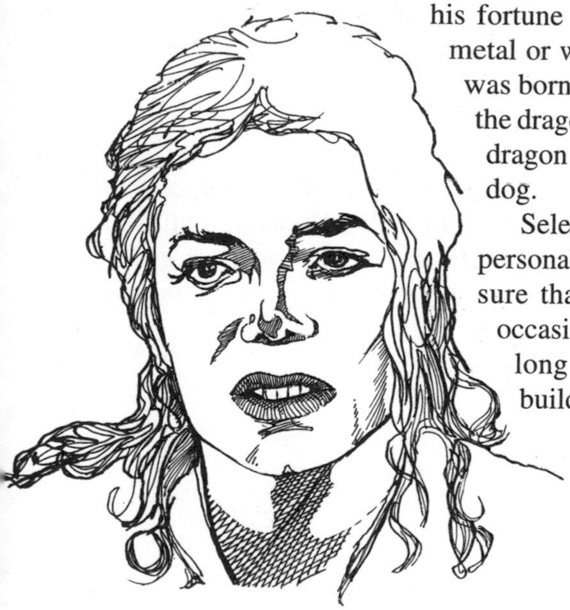

Selecting a good day according to personal favourable elements will ensure that the ceremony or important occasion proceeds smoothly. For the long term prosperity of an office building or shop, a date with elements supportive of the back of the building should be selected. This may sound strange but the Chinese consider the back as the foundation and support of a building or business venture. So if the back of the building is in the east, belonging to the element of wood, then one can choose a day of water as water provides support to the wood. This is particularly important if the building is constructed on open ground without tall buildings or mountains behind its back, symbolising a lack of solid support or backup from behind. Using the same logic, a building without sufficient open space in front needs a day with the element supportive to its front. If such a building faces west and the west is blocked by other buildings, symbolising inadequate prosperity in money terms, one can choose a date of earth for the opening ceremony. The reason is that earth supports metal—a symbol of the direction west.

I have mentioned earlier that the art of date selection involves knowledge from many different branches of Chinese metaphysics and that its techniques are very meticulous. Thus far, I have only applied the knowledge of the Four Pillars of Destiny. However, a knowledge of *feng shui* is equally vital to performing a good task. As discussed in previous chapters, the office is influenced by the changing flying stars of the year, month and day. To ensure that the ceremony proceeds smoothly, it is necessary to note the position of certain bad flying stars. For example, the presence of bad flying star "5 yellow" at the main entrance will bring trouble. Therefore, days or months when the 5 yellow is in the direction of the main entrance or in the direction of the boss's room ought to be avoided.

The yearly, monthly and daily locations of the flying stars are also indicated in the *Tung Shing*.

The Tian Tan Buddha Opening Ceremony

Taking another example, the date 29 December 1993 was selected for the ribbon-cutting ceremony for the giant Tian Tan Buddha statue built in Lantau island. This was an important event attended by thousands of guests and monks from many countries. The date, expressed in terms of the Four Pillars, is:

The Date for the Opening Ceremony

Hour	Day	Month	Year
辛	甲	甲	癸
Metal	Wood	Wood	Water
未	申	子	酉
Earth	Metal	Water	Metal

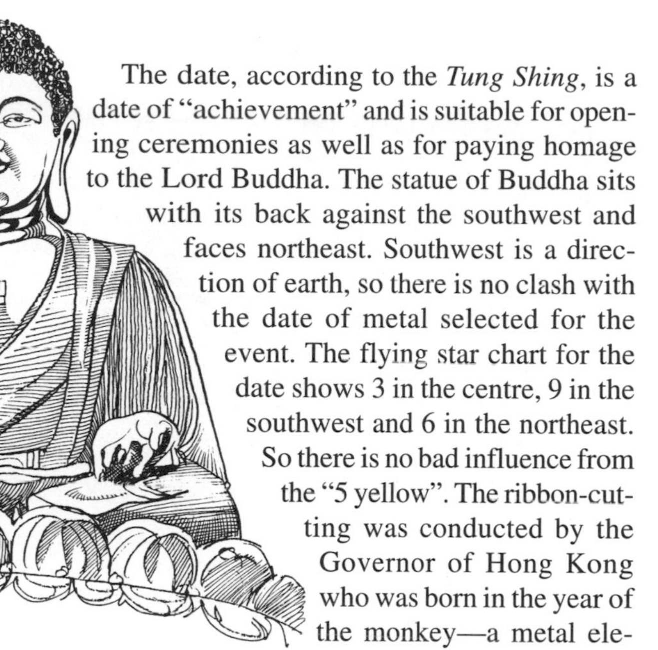

The date, according to the *Tung Shing*, is a date of "achievement" and is suitable for opening ceremonies as well as for paying homage to the Lord Buddha. The statue of Buddha sits with its back against the southwest and faces northeast. Southwest is a direction of earth, so there is no clash with the date of metal selected for the event. The flying star chart for the date shows 3 in the centre, 9 in the southwest and 6 in the northeast. So there is no bad influence from the "5 yellow". The ribbon-cutting was conducted by the Governor of Hong Kong who was born in the year of the monkey—a metal element. Hence, the earthly branch of the date did not clash with his animal sign.

Although I am not an expert on Buddhist events, I believe there were many other reasons this date was chosen. The lack of a fire element in the date may be a drawback though. As the day pillar is wood and the ceremony is held in winter, according to the principle that winter wood needs the warmth of the sun, an hour with a fire element on the heavenly stem should perhaps have been chosen. However, the organizers may have had to take into account other constraints such as the most convenient timing, avoiding clashes in other earthly branches of the date, avoiding clashes with the birth year of important guests and other programme arrangements. Thus we may not always be able to select the best hour and need to make compromises.

This chapter has provided some basic knowledge in selecting a good day to conduct a business occasion. The technique is useful for business people who wish to ensure that certain important occasions, such as contract negotiations, court hearings, opening ceremonies or contract signings, are conducted in an advantageous and trouble-free day. A well-selected date often provides the driving energy for a person to conduct business with high spirit, and will also contribute to the long term success of a business venture.

Using The I Ching Oracle To Help Make Decisions

So far, I have taken you on a trip through the fascinating world of Chinese destiny analysis and *feng shui*. The former allows one to realise one's inborn potential and provides a preview of the future passage through life; the latter is a technique to exploit the environment to enhance our fortune and reduce the probability and intensity of setbacks and mishaps in life. Both these subjects have very important applications in business. The Four Pillars of Destiny provides a reliable tool for forecasting and decision making while *feng shui* enables one to generate more prosperity out of the business environment. Mastering both techniques will greatly enhance our chances of profitability. So what more do we need?

Suppose you have become an expert in using the Four Pillars of Destiny and *feng shui*. You can reasonably figure out your own up and down cycles. You also know how to make adjustments to your environment to enhance prosperity and avoid obstacles. Is this enough to run a successful business? The Four Pillars of Destiny and *feng shui* can offer answers to many problems about business prosperity but there are still grey areas where these techniques are inadequate. One such grey area are decisions involving choices. Suppose you have two attractive projects on hand but due to insufficient funds, you can only invest in one. The Four Pillars of Destiny shows you are in a phase of good fortune and that your investment will be rewarding. But the question is—which of these two projects is more rewarding? Neither *feng shui* nor the Four Pillars of Destiny can answer such questions.

There can be occasions when you wish to know certain facts which are not directly related to your own destiny. In such cases, there is no way to obtain the information from the *feng shui* of your house or from your own set of Four Pillars of Destiny. For example, if you wish to know the general trend of oil prices during a certain period of time, neither *feng shui* nor the Four Pillars of Destiny can help. Often, political events can affect your business decisions. Thus, you may want to know, for example, the chances of survival of the British Conservative government in the coming months, or the political stability in Russia, or the outcome of the Sino-British negotiations on the future of Hong Kong. Because all these questions have no direct bearing on your personal destiny, you need another metaphysical tool to find the answers. That tool is the I Ching Oracle.

The Book Of I Ching

The Book of I Ching, or "Book of Changes", is perhaps the most ancient and respected literature in Chinese metaphysics. It has been translated into many Western languages and its wisdom in explaining the universe has fascinated many Western scholars and scientists who have devoted much effort to study and analyse the rich hidden meanings behind the symbols. The I Ching is considered a representation of Oriental wisdom and its symbols have even been adopted by South Korea for its national flag. In recent years, there have been several intensive studies of the I Ching, both within and outside China, with some startling discoveries. It is beyond the scope of this book to go into great detail about the various discoveries but I will just name a few examples.

The basic philosophy of dualism—the yin and the yang embodied in the I Ching Trigram system—is thought to have inspired the binary system in computer technology. The system of combining pairs of trigrams to form 64 hexagrams has also been found to be closely related to the configuration of the DNA. An astronomical scientist discovered a close correlation between the eight trigrams and the planets of the solar system and on this basis, he successfully forecast the discovery of a tenth planet in the solar system in addition to the nine known planets. With the recent enthusiasm among scientists about Oriental wisdom, the I Ching has also been linked to subjects like quantum mechanics and the search for a unified field theory. With the growing popularity of Oriental mysticism, we will certainly discover more about the true meaning and purpose of the I Ching in the days to come.

The original form of the I Ching is believed to contain only eight trigrams created by a Chinese god or sage called Fu Shi over 10,000 years ago. The eight trigrams refer to eight symbols created by continuous lines, representing the yang (the positive or male), and broken lines, representing the yin (the negative or female).

Three broken or continuous lines can be combined to form a trigram of three lines. In total, eight symbols of three line trigrams can be formed out of all the combinations of continuous and broken lines. Hence we have the famous Eight Trigrams which is the original and most basic form of the I Ching.

Fig. 38 The Eight Trigrams (Early Arrangement)

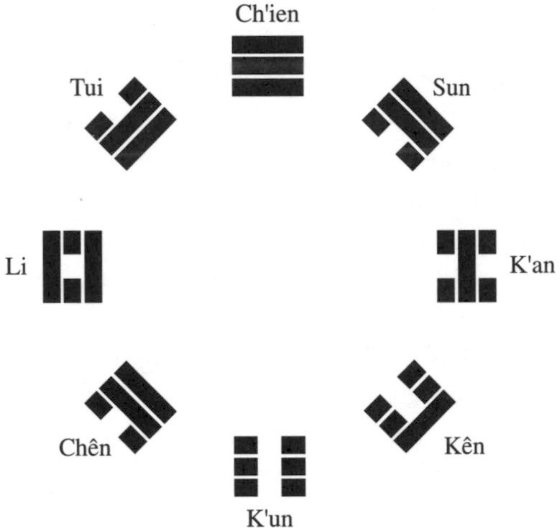

Ch'ien
Tui
Sun
Li
K'an
Chên
Kên
K'un

It was said that the god Fu Shi created the Eight Trigrams from his observations of the heaven and the earth. So each trigram represents an aspect of nature and the Eight Trigrams are believed to be a simplified model of the universe embracing all the essential qualities and orders of the nature or the universe. The basic meanings of the eight trigrams are "Heaven", "Water", "Mountain", "Thunder", "Wind", "Fire", "Earth" and "Lake", which appears to cover all the essential objects on earth during prehistoric days. Subsequently, as human society became more complex, the meanings of the Eight Trigrams were expanded. Meanings related to human relationships, the human body, various animals, shapes, colours and trades were added to the trigrams.

Gradually, it became obvious that the eight symbols were inadequate to contain more refined meaning. So, in order to represent more complex matters in human society like feelings, relations, and even human fortune, pairs of trigrams were put together to form hexagrams. By exhausting the combinations of any two trigrams, one can obtain a total of 64 different hexagrams. Hence the information capacity of the hexagrams is considerably more than the Eight Trigrams and almost any object or event in the universe can be represented by these symbols of six lines.

Fig. 39 A sample hexagram

As the symbols are supposed to hold all the information about the universe, one major application of these symbols in the ancient days was for forecasting. It became a tool for Oracle purposes, providing hints about the future so that the ancient Chinese could follow some kind of guidelines to choose the right path of action. In ancient Chinese history, the I Ching has frequently been used as a tool for Oracles; records show how many nobles and kings through the years relied on the I Ching Oracle to make decisions regarding politics and warfare.

Besides being a tool for predicting the future, some sages and scholars also found the I Ching an important guide to social relationships and various other aspects of life. They devoted considerable effort to explain each line of the 64 hexagrams and to relate them to human life and philosophy. The I Ching as we see it today actually contains detailed notes and explanations written by Emperor Chou and Confucius. These notes contain their wisdom in interpreting the hexagrams and are an excellent reference for understanding the philosophical meanings of the symbols. Today, many still rely on these explanations to perform the I Ching Oracle, that is, ask questions and receive answers about the future.

I will not delve deeper into the academic aspect of the I Ching as my main purpose of introducing this famous book here is to show how a businessman can use it as a tool for forecasting. The I Ching Oracle is most useful when we have a specific question in mind or when we are at a crossroads and need to decide which path of action to take. During such moments of hesitation, the I Ching can cast light on uncertainties and provide guidance for making a choice.

To perform an I Ching Oracle is rather easy—all you need are three coins and concentration of mind. However, interpreting the kua (or hexagrams) to obtain the correct answers to your questions is somewhat more difficult.

The chapters that follow will take you through the processes step by step leading to the most effective way of interpreting the kua. This technique is a powerful tool for forecasting and is very useful for problem solving and decision making.

How To Perform An I Ching Oracle

The purpose of performing an I Ching Oracle is to obtain an answer to a question. So the most important step before performing the Oracle is to carefully think over what you want to ask and then try to formulate the question as clearly as possible. Students who have experience practising this kind of Oracle will find that clearer questions bring clearer answers and makes the interpretation of the hexagram much easier. The following are the necessary steps in performing an I Ching Oracle:

Step One—Formulate A Clear Question

In an ordinary consultation, one can raise any questions that come to mind without thinking carefully as there are opportunities to clarify if the question is not clear. However, performing an Oracle is more complicated and you should assume that you have only one chance to ask the question with no further opportunity to follow up. So before asking, one must be clear what he wishes to know as vague questions will receive vague answers. One must also bear in mind that the answer is not provided in words, but in the form of a hexagram which requires much analysis to obtain a meaningful answer to your question.

When interpreting the hexagram, one must constantly recall the question to get a correct answer. If the question is not clear, the meaning of the hexagram will also be vague and the interpretation becomes difficult. Thus, the question should be specific and to the point. Some kind of time frame should also be incorporated into the question so that the answer will be restricted to a certain period of time.

For example, if you want to take part in a joint venture and wish to find out the profitability of such venture, a question like "Shall I put my money into this venture?" lacks clarity at least in two respects. Firstly, it does not specify what aspect you are looking for in such an investment. If your priority is money, you should state so. There can be other non-monetary gains in any venture, such as enhancement of harmony and human relationship, gain in reputation and status or gain in working experience in a certain field of industry. Even if you receive a positive answer from the I Ching, you can't be certain that you will have money gains from the venture.

Secondly, there is no time frame to the question. If you get a positive answer from the hexagram, you are still uncertain when the benefit will come—will it mean benefit in the long run of five years or so? If quick returns are what you are after, you should restrict the time frame to 12 months. The proper way of framing the question should then be "What will be the money profit in the next 12 months if I invest in this project?"

Such a question is clear-cut. Any positive indication by the hexagram can easily be interpreted as short term profitability within a time frame of 12 months.

If monetary profit is not your only concern and you care very much for a harmonious relationship with the partner, then you can ask a second question focusing on human relationship. The question can be "Can I maintain a harmonious working relationship with Mr. A over the next 12 months?" I strongly advise that each Oracle only cover one specific area. Remember that multi-levelled questions will draw multi-levelled answers and complicate the interpretation process.

Step Two—Toss Three Coins

A hexagram is a symbol of six continuous or broken lines. The continuous line is yang; the broken line is yin. Modern scientists often associate them with the binary system which is the foundation of computer science. One can even simply assume yang is 1 and yin is 0 in the binary system. To obtain a hexagram at random, the most convenient method commonly employed is to toss three coins six times, and use the configurations obtained to draw up each of the six lines.

Any common coin with an easily distinguishable head and tail can be used for this exercise. Before tossing the coins, there are a few points to note. Firstly, you should choose a quiet place to perform the Oracle. As concentration of thought is required during the process, you should minimise any possible distractions by making sure the door is locked and the telephone is off the hook. It is also customary to clean one's hands before tossing as such rituals are believed to help concentration of the mind.

The simple tools you need are the three coins, a pen and a note pad to record the hexagram. When everything is ready, focus your mind on the prepared question and begin tossing the coins. When tossing three coins onto the floor, four outcomes are possible. One Head and two Tails, two Heads and one Tail, three Heads, and three Tails. The following diagram shows how to draw up a hexagram with six lines, on the basis of the outcome of the three-coin configurations.

Fig. 40 Obtaining a hexagram from three-coin configurations

Combination of coins			Symbols	
Head	Tail	Tail	———	Yang
Head	Head	Tail	— —	Yin
Head	Head	Head	— — ← ———	Yang changes to Yin
Tail	Tail	Tail	——— ← — —	Yin changes to Yang

If the outcome is one Head, it symbolises a yang or continuous line. Two Heads means a yin or broken line. All Heads and all Tails represent active and changing lines. All Heads means a yang line changing into yin while all Tails means the yin line changing into yang. These active lines indicate where the actions and changes will be and are very important to the interpretation process. After tossing six times and obtaining the outcomes, you should immediately record down the six lines onto the note pad.

Step Three—Label The Hexagram

Now you have a hexagram of six lines, representing the answer to your question. To the layman, the hexagram is merely a picture of lines without meaning. Thus, one has to go through the process of labelling the hexagram before carrying out the interpretation to decipher the hidden meaning of the hexagram.

At this juncture, it is necessary to explain that there are two common practices of interpreting the meaning of an I Ching hexagram. One practice, which I call the academic school, is simply to look up the book of I Ching and check the meaning of the hexagram. This practice is common among academics and most Western literature about the I Ching have adopted this method.

However, this is a difficult way in two senses. Firstly, the explanations in the book were written by Confucius and Emperor Chou who lived about 3,000 years ago. Society then was very different from our world today, so it is not easy to associate the explanations with our questions. Secondly, the writings of Emperor Chou and Confucius were very philosophical and mostly emphasise social aspects; they may not embrace the wide scope of meanings originally intended for the trigrams. As such, relying on the book of I Ching to interpret a hexagram requires considerable imagination and a subjective view to relate the explanations to today's world. The same hexagram may even draw conflicting conclusions if interpreted by two different persons.

There is another method of interpreting the hexagrams, which is commonly employed by professional fortune-tellers. This practice does not rely on the book of I Ching but employs the basic theory of the five elements to draw conclusions from the hexagram. The method is to label each line with elements, evaluate the interrelationships and strengths of each line according to the elements, and then draw a conclusion. The process includes weighing and balancing the elements in each line, similar to the analysis of the Four Pillars of Destiny.

This practice is commonly adopted by fortune-tellers for two reasons. Firstly, as mentioned earlier, the book of I Ching in its present form contains the personal viewpoints of Confucius and Emperor Chou and their viewpoints were not necessarily the only correct interpretations. Secondly, the labelling method can clearly classify each line and each element into five aspects of life, including money, status, authority, aspirations and colleagues. Such classification enables one to easily relate the hexagram to real life problems.

The trigrams were in existence long before the Chou dynasty and Confucius. So the practice of performing the Oracle by the trigrams and hexagrams were common long before the book of I Ching was compiled around the time of the Chou dynasty and the age of the warring states. My preference is to use the labelling method which is more creative and effective.

There are four steps involved in labelling a hexagram. To do this you need to refer to the tables in Appendix 9 of this book.

Step 1 Identify the kua element. Each hexagram can be identified with one element.

Step 2 Label the elements against each line. There are a total of 64 hexagrams and the elements of each line are fixed. Appendix 9 shows you the elemental labels for each line for all 64 hexagrams.

Step 3 Mark the subject line and the object line. Out of the six lines of a hexagram, one should be labelled object and another, subject. The correct positions of these two lines can also be found in Appendix 9. In general, the subject line represents the person asking the question while the object line is the matter being asked.

Step 4 Label the aspects against each line. There are altogether five aspects of life which can be derived from the relationship between the kua element (see Step 1), and the element of each line. These five aspects are money, status, aspirations, authority and colleagues. The process of deriving these aspects is similar to deriving different aspects of life from a set of Four Pillars of Destiny.

The following table shows how they are derived:

Relations between kua element and line element	**Aspects of line element**
Kua element same as line element	Colleagues
Kua element destroys line element	Money
Kua element gives birth to line element	Aspiration
Kua element is given birth by line element	Authority
Kua element is destroyed by line element	Power status

All one needs to do is to familiarise oneself with the Cycle of Birth and Cycle of Destruction of the five elements. For example, if the kua element is wood, a line of wood will symbolise colleagues, a line of earth will symbolise money as wood destroys earth, and a line of fire will represent aspiration as fire is generated from wood. Lines of water and metal will symbolise authority, and power and status, respectively.

Step Four—Interpretation

This is the most crucial part of the Oracle process as one needs to decipher the meaning of the hexagram after it has been obtained and properly labelled. The process is similar to analysing a set of Four Pillars of Destiny. The next few chapters will illustrate how we can correctly interpret a hexagram to answer our questions.

RISK ANALYSIS THROUGH HEXAGRAMS

There are altogether 64 different hexagrams in the I Ching. However, this does not mean that we can only expect 64 possible results from tossing three coins. The reason is that we can have active lines when we get three Heads or three Tails and such active lines can occur on each of the six lines of any hexagram.

Furthermore, each hexagram can have more than one active line. Hence the number of possible hexagrams that can be obtained by tossing three coins is enormous. To add to the complexity, the same hexagram can be interpreted differently according to the nature of the question. So the answers that one can obtain from the I Ching Oracle is almost limitless. There is no boundary to the type of questions one can ask. We can obtain, through the I Ching Oracle, hints about anything in the universe, as long as we know the right question to ask.

As the answers to everything in the universe can be represented by the simple kua—a hexagram of six lines—we can imagine that the answers are presented in a very symbolic and abstract manner. Interpreting the hexagrams to obtain the right answer is no easy task and requires much practice and experience before one can achieve a high standard of accuracy. The fastest path to becoming a good prophet is to be confident and to trust one's own logical mind as the interpretations rely only on some very simple rules. The rest is purely logical deduction.

In the last chapter, I have illustrated how to fully label a hexagram. After completing the step of labelling, we now have in front of us the answer to our question in the form of a hexagram. The process of interpretation can then begin.

The first item to examine is the line marked "subject". For most questions, there is usually someone who does the asking. The subject line is the symbol of the person who asks the question. If you ask something about yourself, then it represents you. If your friend requests you to ask a question about him, then the subject line represents your friend. The other five lines symbolise the circumstances or matters surrounding the question. Thus, the strength and situation of the subject line is very important and provides many hints to answer your question. If you want to know whether a project will be successful, the subject line represents you, the project manager or the investor, and the other lines represent the environment surrounding you and the project.

A strong subject line means you are capable of controlling your environment and often indicates success. On the other hand, a very weak subject line indicates weakness and you may encounter obstacles and failure. It is essential to determine whether the subject line is strong or weak. The strength of the subject line is affected by two main factors. Firstly, the timing of the Oracle will show whether the element of the subject line is in a prosperous or weak season. For example, if one performs an I Ching Oracle in the winter season in a month of water, a subject line of water will be a strong line as water is most prosperous in winter. On the other hand, a subject line of fire is very weak as fire is suppressed by water in winter.

The second factor affecting the strength of the subject line is the active line. Active lines refer to those lines changing from yang to yin or from yin to yang when you get all three Heads or all three Tails. These are very important lines as they indicate where the changes and actions in your environment will be. All these changes will cast an effect on the subject line and will reflect how the environment reacts to your action. Some react to give the subject line strong support while others react to suppress the subject line.

Take, for example, the subject line of water. Water needs the support of metal, so an active line of metal will provide support to the water. The support will be very strong if the active line of metal changes into earth, as earth, in turn, generates support to the metal. What if the metal line changes not to earth but to fire? Since fire suppresses metal, the support from the metal line will be weak. We therefore have to examine the changes of these active lines and see what effect they will have on the subject line. If the question is about the prospect of your project, the active lines will help determine whether you will gain support or rejection from surrounding people or your environment.

In most cases, knowing the strength of the subject line and the support of the active lines will be enough for you to come to a conclusion. However, if your question requires more details, you can continue to dig deeper to uncover more information from the hexagram.

Sometimes you do not just wish to know the success or failure of a project—you also want to know in what respect it succeeds or fails. To answer such questions, you can examine the labels regarding the different aspects of life—money, status, authority, aspiration and colleagues. If the project is a commercial venture, it is logical to examine the lines labelled money and evaluate its strength as though you are evaluating the subject line above. If the line labelled as money is weak, then obviously the project will not bring much money profit.

Investing In A Movie

To illustrate the process of interpreting an I Ching Oracle, let me demonstrate with the following example. On 6 August 1993, I performed an I Ching Oracle for a friend who had been invited by a film director to invest in an international movie scheduled for release in the next few months. The question I asked was "Will his investment in this movie project bring him money profit in the next 12 months?" I obtained the following hexagram after tossing my three coins six times.

Fig. 41 Kua revealing the profitability of a film project

(Aspiration) Wood ______	(Status) Earth	__ __		
	(Resources) Metal	__ __	Subject	
(Status) Earth __ __	(Money) Fire	______		
				Kua Element: Water
	(Colleague) Water	______		
	(Status) Earth	__ __	Object	
	(Aspiration) Wood	______		

One has to remember that it is customary to read a hexagram from bottom up. The bottom line is thus called the first line or line one, the second line from the bottom is called the second line, and so on.

The hexagram is fully labelled with subject, object, elements and aspects. Let us examine the subject line first. It is a line of metal and represents my friend. As the Oracle was performed in the summer season, the prosperous element is fire, not metal. So it is not a strong subject line.

Next we see if the subject line can gain some support from the active lines. There is an active line of earth on top (the sixth line). Earth is the mother of metal, so this line supports the subject line of metal. However, this earth line changes into wood, and wood destroys earth. Thus such an earth line cannot support the subject.

As the question also asks about money profit, we should examine the money aspect of this hexagram too. The fourth line from bottom is labelled as a money line and this line is active and changing. The money line is of the fire element, which changes into the earth element. According to the cycle of birth, fire gives birth to earth, so earth will exhaust the strength of the fire. Therefore this active line reflects a reduction in money, rather than money prosperity.

This hexagram indicated that the investment would not be profitable and that my friend would not make any money out of the project over the next 12 months.

How To Forecast World Events

Obtaining a hexagram by the tossing of coins is easy to learn. However, getting a hexagram is merely the beginning of the task—the most critical part of an I Ching Oracle is to interpret the hexagram correctly to get the right answer to your question.

There are some basic rules in analysing a hexagram. The fundamental step is to evaluate the strength of the subject line, which symbolises the subject matter or the person asking the question. A strong subject line, in most situations, reflects a person who is in a position of strength, with a greater chance of achieving his goal.

For other questions which cover special aspects of life, such as money, status or position, one can find these aspects by correctly labelling each line. For example, if the question is about money, then one should look for the line symbolising money and evaluate its strength. However, note that money still needs to be controlled by the person. So a very prominent line of money requires a strong subject line to keep it under control. A strong money line but weak subject line may indicate a heavy burden related to money rather than profit making.

Another important item to note is the active line. Active lines point to areas of changes and actions and one should examine whether these changes are supportive or detrimental to the subject line. This can be decisive in one's analysis about the strength of the subject line and hence the direction that the hexagram is pointing.

In the section about the Four Pillars of Destiny, we have learned that the prosperity of the five elements is cyclical. This is very important in determining the strength of each of the lines in a hexagram. The following table shows how each of the five elements prosper and die during the four seasons of a year:

	Spring	**Summer**	**Autumn**	**Winter**
Metal	die	born	prosper	weak
Wood	prosper	weak	die	born
Water	weak	die	born	prosper
Fire	born	prosper	weak	die
Earth	prosper in every third month of a season			

The table shows that a line labelled with a particular element varies in strength according to the month and season when the Oracle is performed. For example, if the line in question is fire and the Oracle is performed in winter when fire is dying, the strength of this fire line is automatically discounted. So it is absolutely necessary to take the season into consideration when evaluating the strength of any line in a hexagram.

These are just some general guidelines. It is impossible to cover all the possible questions we can pose to the I Ching, so we has to exercise our imagination to retrieve as much information as possible from a hexagram. The technique can be improved upon and polished considerably with more practice.

In the last chapter we have seen an example of using the I Ching Oracle to predict the profitability of taking part in a business venture. This is an example of using the I Ching Oracle for individual decision making. However, the technique is certainly not restricted to such a small scope. There are occasions when we need to forecast future events of a macro scale to assist our business decisions. An entrepreneur who is contemplating buying or chartering a ship to transport his cargo may need to forecast macro matters like the prosperity of the world shipping market, the trend of fuel oil prices or the atmosphere of the global economy. To obtain hints on such matters, the I Ching Oracle may be the only reliable tool in metaphysics.

Why Beijing Lost Its Bid For The 2000 Olympics

Assuming an investor is about to make a decision on whether to invest in Beijing and wishes to know the chances of Beijing being selected to host the 2000 Olympics. He can pose this question to the I Ching Oracle.

On 20 September 1993, just three days before the voting by the Olympic Committee to decide on the issue, I asked the following question: "What are Beijing's chances of hosting the 2000 Olympics?", and the following hexagram was obtained by tossing three coins.

Fig. 42 Kua revealing Beijing's chances of hosting the Olympic Games in 2000

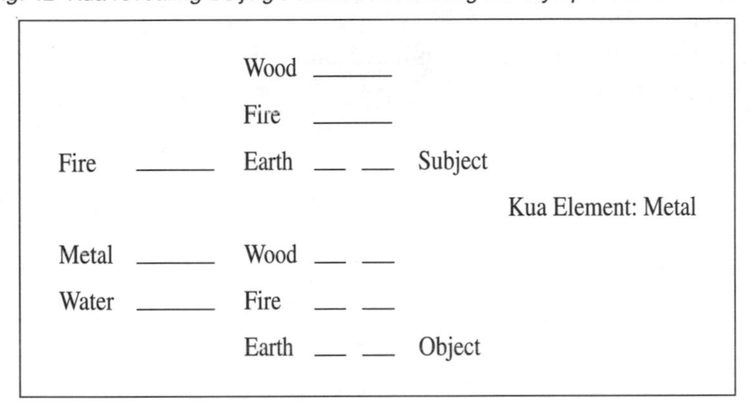

Let us first examine the subject line which symbolises Beijing. It is occupied by a line of earth. The Oracle was performed in September 1993 which was a season of metal in a year of metal. Metal exhausts the energy of earth, so the subject line is not very strong. However, it is an active line of earth, transforming into fire. Fire gives birth and support to earth, so the subject line is strengthened. But again, we must not neglect to look at the season to determine whether the fire support is strong enough. As the Oracle was performed in autumn, a season of metal, again the fire power is weak. Thus, the picture is that although Beijing—symbolised by the subject line of earth—has been putting in a lot of effort to apply to host the 2000 Games, the circumstance was unfavourable.

After evaluating the subject line, we need to examine the other active lines to see if there exists any strong support from other lines. In this case, we can see that, besides the subject line, there are two other active lines—fire and wood. As the subject line is earth, an active line of fire means there is external support. However, this line of fire transforms into water which extinguishes the fire. Hence this support is weakened and fails to take effect. The other active line is wood transforming into metal which destroys wood. So again, this wood fails to deliver any favourable impact.

In balance, the subject line (symbolising Beijing) is weak in this hexagram and external support is inadequate. It points to the conclusion that Beijing's chances of success are slim. Eventually, on 23 September 1993, Sydney was elected as the city to host the Olympic Games in 2000. Beijing narrowly lost out by two votes. This was clearly indicated in the above hexagram. Although the subject line of earth was not too weak and was supported by fire, its strength was insufficient as both earth and fire were not "in season" in September.

More practical examples to enhance our techniques will be given in the following chapters.

Chance Analysis For Contract Bidding

In the business world, dealing with challenges and competition is a daily affair. Marketing people especially, invariably encounter strong competition for any attractive business deal. Faced with a strong competitor when bidding for a business contract, one not only needs to know one's own capability but also the opponent's strength and potential before making the best possible bid. There are several ways to achieve this goal. Most marketing managers rely on market intelligence and their experience. Even so, there will be surprises, wrong estimations, misleading intelligence and other unknown factors that can cause the most capable marketing team to stumble. So the factor of luck and chance still plays an important role in such business negotiations.

As mentioned in previous chapters, the I Ching Oracle is a technique that allows us to gaze into the unknown future. The process is simple and accuracy can be startlingly high. So there is little to lose and everything to gain by using the Oracle as another management tool to help one's judgements and decisions.

If we expect a strong competitor when bidding for an attractive business deal, we need to find out our chances of success relative to the competitor. This is a simple question and we can perform an I Ching Oracle to obtain the answer within minutes.

Supposing we ask the following question on 18 October 1993—"What are our chances of clinching the business contract in 1993, as compared to our competitor?"

The following hexagram was obtained by tossing three coins.

Fig. 43 Kua revealing the strength of a competitor

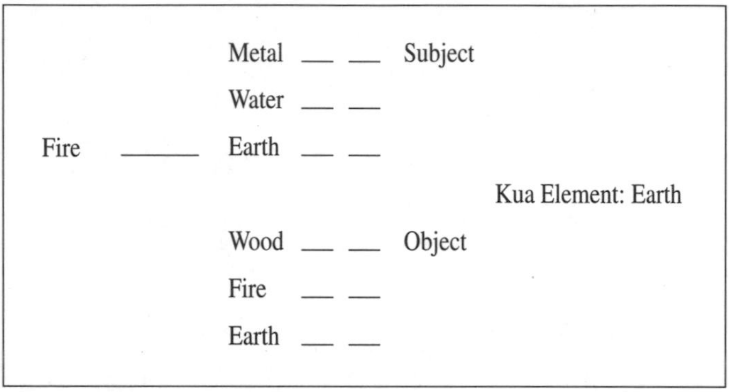

		Metal	— —	Subject
		Water	— —	
Fire	——	Earth	— —	
				Kua Element: Earth
		Wood	— —	Object
		Fire	— —	
		Earth	— —	

The interpretation for this hexagram is relatively simple. One should assume the subject line to represent the self, and the object line to represent the competitor. With this in mind, the task of interpretation is merely to compare the strength of these two lines and evaluate which is stronger. If the subject line is stronger, then you have a better chance of winning. A very strong object line but weak subject line indicates a strong competitor and your chances of winning the business are slim.

When evaluating the strength of the subject line and object line, you should consider the following factors. Firstly, you need to see if the element represented by the line is in season. For example, a metal line will be strongest if the Oracle is performed in autumn and will be weak if performed in summer. Then you have to take note of the active lines. These active lines reflect actions and changes, and will affect the strength of the subject or object line. The active lines often symbolise some other people or factor at play which will either help one party to win or create an obstacle to the deal.

For example, if the subject line is metal, and there is an active line of earth changing to fire, then the active line is a supportive force. The reason is that fire supports earth, and earth supports metal. So an active line of earth changing into fire means the earth is very strong (with fire's support) and can give strong assistance to the metal. The metal subject line—symbolising the self—is then likely to win. If, on the other hand, the active line is earth changing into wood, it means that the earth is trying to assist the metal subject line but fails because the earth is suppressed by the wood. This is because wood destroys earth.

If the active line is not earth, but fire changing into wood, then the fire is very strong with the wood support and such strong fire will destroy the metal subject line. This reflects strong opposition or obstacles to the self in bidding for the project and you should consider withdrawing to save both effort and expense.

One can repeat the evaluation for the object line and see whether the object line is in season and whether there are any active lines in its favour or reducing its strength. After evaluating both the subject and object lines, it will not be difficult to come to a conclusion as to which party possesses a better chance of winning.

Let us now return to the sample Oracle we obtained on 18 October 1993. The hexagram shows a subject line of metal—representing the self. As October is a month of earth in the autumn season, and metal is supposed to be prosperous in autumn, we can conclude that the metal subject line is fairly strong, being "in season". The next step is to examine the active lines. There is only a single active line in the hexagram. This is a line of earth changing to fire. Earth is the supporter of metal, and fire is the supporter of earth. So an earth line changing to fire reflects very strong earth, symbolising that the metal subject line will receive strong support in the bid.

After looking at the strength of the self (the subject line), let us examine the opponent—the object line. It is a line of wood which is quite weak in the autumn season. The reason is that autumn is a month of prevailing metal influence and metal is the destroyer of wood. Moreover, the year 1993—the year of the Rooster—is a year of metal which also threatens the wood. Weak wood requires watering to survive. Although there is a water line in the upper hexagram, it is not active and cannot provide support to the wood object line. It is obvious then that this wood object line is weak.

With such an imbalanced strength between the subject line and the object line, we can confidently predict that the self—symbolised by the strong subject line—will win this contest.

The process described above is not overly complicated and with a little practice, one can easily learn to employ it as an economical and handy management tool.

How Much Destiny Is Predetermined?

Many Chinese emperors over the past 6,000 years of recorded history relied heavily on cosmology and metaphysical methods to rule the country. The ancient methods of the I Ching Oracle were used for important policy decisions as early as 4000 B.C., and more evidence of the vast employment of such techniques has been discovered by archaeologists in recent years. This tradition lasted until the fall of the Ching Dynasty when the Chinese realised they had fallen far behind the Western sciences. The ancient Chinese traditions were then temporarily put aside. However, after several decades of modernization to catch up with the West, there now appears to be a growing trend of reviving the treasures of ancient Chinese knowledge. This knowledge is not only as useful in our daily lives as Western sciences, it can, in many respects, supplement Western shortcomings.

A good example is Chinese herbal medicine and acupuncture. Many people are discovering that Western medicine may not have all the answers and finding out that Chinese medical practices, built on a theory of internal balance and harmony of the five elements and the yin and yang, can perhaps offer a better chance for curing some diseases caused by an imbalanced metabolism within our bodies. Combining both Western and Oriental techniques may thus be a practical solution to improve the standard of medical care.

In managerial sciences, the Japanese style of management and the Chinese Suen Tsu martial strategy have become increasingly popular. However, these merely brush the surface of Oriental knowledge. I do not see why the Chinese metaphysical methods which were employed by emperors and sages to formulate their national policies cannot be integrated into the modern management style as well. Chinese metaphysics advocates harmony with the universe. It not only offers a deeper understanding of the Oriental mind but also provides a key for managers to gaze into future trends so that they can make more effective decisions. In the dynamic and highly competitive commercial world of today, managers can only survive by keeping one step ahead of others. However, this step must be taken in the right direction and Chinese metaphysical tools can be regarded as the compass revealing the most appropriate way.

The use of tools like *feng shui* and the Four Pillars of Destiny in business may sound bold and revolutionary to Western ears. However, many successful billionaires and entrepreneurs among the Chinese community in Hong Kong, Taiwan and Southeast Asia are believed to consult *feng shui* experts when decorating their offices, selecting an auspicious date for important events or evaluating their risks in business ventures. If an entrepreneur uses metaphysical consultations, he will find it worthwhile to acquire some knowledge of the subject and incorporate the technique into his management system.

The advantage of learning, instead of consulting, is that a businessman with a business background understands his risks better than a *feng shui* man who may not possess any business training. Deriving your own conclusion from the metaphysical signs may thus be more reliable.

A book about metaphysical methods and destiny analysis cannot be complete without a discourse on the paradox between freewill and destiny. If we believe in destiny, it implies that all is predetermined and there is not much freewill. Whether this is true or not, there are considerable objections against taking such an attitude towards life. For one, this is not positive thinking. Moreover, it implies that we are not responsible for what we do. However, such determinism is not difficult to appreciate. We are a tiny part of the universe and the universe is subject to fixed rules and orders. So human fate and destiny is, in fact, determined by the universal order which is irresistible.

Stephen Hawking's Conclusion

This view is also accepted by modern scientists. In his essay "Is Everything Determined?", the brilliant British scientist Mr. Stephen Hawking concluded that everything is governed by the set of physical rules of the universe. However, we cannot predict the details only because the equations are so complicated that it is not possible for us to solve them all. As such, it is more appropriate to act as if life is not predetermined since it is not possible to know what has been determined for us.

From the viewpoint of Chinese metaphysics, everything in the universe must follow a set of rules and such rules determine our fate. Therefore, by understanding the mechanism of these rules, we can better understand our destiny. This is similar to Mr. Hawking's view. The main difference is that the tools we employ, such as the Four Pillars of Destiny, are not as complicated as scientific equations. Still, these tools have considerable limitations. For example, the Four Pillars of Destiny is able to tell a wealthy person from his birth data, but it cannot predict how much money he will own. Will he be just a millionaire or will he be as rich as Mr. Li Ka-shing? So while the Four Pillars of Destiny is able to portray a fortune profile of ups and downs corresponding to phases in life, it is impossible to predict how much we will achieve during the fortunate phase of life or how hard we will fall during periods of misfortune.

Another argument against predetermined destiny is that in a monumental event such as the Hiroshima atomic explosion that killed thousands of people at the same moment, certainly not all the victims' pillars of destiny reflected such sudden death. Therefore, the individual destiny must be subject to the larger destiny of the land.

I believe that the Four Pillars of Destiny is merely one of several equations that can cast light on human destiny. There are other variables, such as *feng shui*, the fortune of the land, individual effort and, of course, freewill, which affect our fate. The solution offered by the Four Pillars of Destiny is therefore not one hundred per cent accurate.

I completely agree with Mr. Hawking's view that believing in freewill is more appropriate as long as there is no absolutely accurate method of predicting the future down to minor details. However, the other extreme—counting everything on freewill—is also unrealistic. After all, we know that not all effort is rewarded and that hard work does not always gain good results. So it becomes necessary to understand that mysterious variable at play, commonly known as luck. The Four Pillars of Destiny tells us that luck is not a random factor and that it follows a predictable pattern. Mastering the pattern of luck will enable us to put our efforts to more rewarding use.

In time travel stories, there always seems to be an episode where the hero travels into the past and takes some action that changes his present or future, making it appear that destiny is changeable. Moreover, the purpose of learning about destiny is to understand and improve our destiny. If destiny can be changed, is it paradoxical to say that destiny is predictable? To address this challenge, I think we should distinguish carefully between "changing" destiny and "improving" destiny.

Changing destiny refers to turning misfortune into good luck, which I consider impossible and as difficult as attempting to resist the universal order. However, improving destiny means that we reduce our losses during a down phase and improve our gains during a period of good luck. I do not think this is against the universal order. Neither is this paradoxical to the concept that destiny is foreseeable.

All the metaphysical tools I have introduced in this book aim for this ultimate goal—to improve our destiny by obtaining a clearer view of our future.

APPENDIX 1

HOW TO CONVERT THE WESTERN CALENDAR INTO THE FOUR PILLARS OF DESTINY

In most methods of destiny analysis, a person's fortune is identified by his birth data, which is regarded as some sort of cosmic code, able to reveal the components of our destiny. The Four Pillars of Destiny method also constructs our destiny on the basis of individual birth data, which includes the birth year, month, day and hour. This data is translated into the five basic elements—metal, wood, water, fire and earth through the Chinese calendar. Therefore, the first step to practising the Four Pillars of Destiny is to translate a set of birth data from the Western calendar into the Chinese calendar.

The tool to perform this exercise is a book called *The Thousand Years Almanac*. It contains the conversion tables between the Western calendar and the Chinese calendar, usually covering about 130 years between 1900 to 2030. This book enables us to convert any Western calendar into the form of heavenly stems and earthly branches.

The first step to using the calendar is to find the page covering the relevant year. For example, let us translate the following data into the Four Pillars:

Year – 1993
Month – December
Day – 13th
Hour – 10 a.m.

Turn to the page showing the calendar for the year 1993. In the first column, you will be able to see the large Chinese characters "癸酉". These two characters represent the pillar for the year 1993.

Each column shows dates in Arabic numbers. Find the Arabic number 12/13 and you will also see the two Chinese characters "戊辰" in the same box containing "12/13".

These two Chinese characters represent the day pillar. We have now obtained the year and day pillars.

The next step is to find out which month the date 12/13 falls into so that we can establish the month pillar as well. This is somewhat more complicated as each vertical column of *The Thousand Years Almanac* shows a month in the Chinese Lunar calendar, which is different from the Hsia calendar adopted for the Four Pillars of Destiny. Therefore the commencing date on each vertical column (the box on top) is only the commencing date of the month in the lunar calendar, which is not applicable here. We need to find the commencing date in the Hsia calendar instead.

The commencing date for each month of the Hsia calendar is marked in black boxes. As our date is 12/13, we shall look back to see which is the black box prior to the date 12/13. In this example, we can see that the date 12/7 is marked in black. So 12/7 is the commencing date for the month. And 1/5 is the starting date of the following month. Hence the month in which the date 12/13 falls into is a month which starts on 12/7 and ends at 1/5.

Looking up the top of the column, one can find the Chinese character "甲子" which represents the month pillar for the date 12/13.

One complication is that there are two black boxes for each month. One shows the beginning of a month while the other shows the midpoint of a month. We therefore have to be careful not to take the midpoint of the month by mistake. The key to distinguishing between the starting date and the mid date is that the starting date often falls in the range between the 1st and the 10th of the Western calendar. So a blackened date after the 10th is likely to be the mid month date, not the starting date.

Now we have the year pillar, the month pillar and the day pillar. The remaining task is to find the hour pillar. The Chinese divide the time of each day into 12 hours, represented by the 12 earthly branches. The following table shows the conversion between the Chinese hour and the Western hour. One can easily look up this table to convert Western time into Chinese hours. In our example, 10 a.m. in the table is represented by the Chinese character " 巳 ". So this is the earthly branch of the hour pillar.

Western Time	Chinese Hour	Animal Signs
2300 – 0100	子	Rat
0100 – 0300	丑	Ox
0300 – 0500	寅	Tiger
0500 – 0700	卯	Rabbit
0700 – 0900	辰	Dragon
0900 – 1100	巳	Snake
1100 – 1300	午	Horse
1300 – 1500	未	Goat
1500 – 1700	申	Monkey
1700 – 1900	酉	Rooster
1900 – 2100	戌	Dog
2100 – 2300	亥	Pig

We have now established the year, month, day and hour pillars for the moment of time 10 a.m., 13 December 1993 as follows:

Hour	Day	Month	Year
?	戊 Earth	甲 Wood	癸 Water
巳 Fire	辰 Earth	子 Water	酉 Metal

However, these steps only provide seven Chinese characters. The heavenly stem of the hour pillar is still missing. The method to find the heavenly stems of the hour pillar is given in the following appendix.

APPENDIX 2

HOW TO FIND THE HEAVENLY STEM FOR AN HOUR PILLAR

The heavenly stem of the hour pillar is determined by the heavenly stem of the day pillar:

Day Pillars		Heavenly Stem of 1st Hour
甲 Yang Wood	己 Yin Earth	甲 Yang Wood
乙 Yin Wood	庚 Yang Metal	丙 Yang Fire
丙 Yang Fire	辛 Yin Metal	戊 Yang Earth
丁 Yin Fire	壬 Yang Water	庚 Yang Metal
戊 Yang Earth	癸 Yin Water	壬 Yang Water

After finding the first hour heavenly stem from the above table, you can locate the remaining 11 hour heavenly stems by counting forward. For example, if the day heavenly stem is yang metal 庚:

Hour	Stem	Branch	Time
1st hour —	丙 Fire	子 Water	(2300 – 0100)
2nd hour —	丁 Fire	丑 Earth	(0100 – 0300)
3rd hour —	戊 Earth	寅 Wood	(0300 – 0500)
4th hour —	己 Earth	卯 Wood	(0500 – 0700)
5th hour —	庚 Metal	辰 Earth	(0700 – 0900)
6th hour —	辛 Metal	巳 Fire	(0900 – 1100)
7th hour —	壬 Water	午 Fire	(1100 – 1300)
8th hour —	癸 Water	未 Earth	(1300 – 1500)
9th hour —	甲 Wood	申 Metal	(1500 – 1700)
10th hour —	乙 Wood	酉 Metal	(1700 – 1900)
11th hour —	丙 Fire	戌 Earth	(1900 – 2100)
12th hour —	丁 Fire	亥 Water	(2100 – 2300)

APPENDIX 3

HOW TO LIST OUT THE LUCK PILLARS

Luck pillars are double Chinese characters derived from the month pillar. They represent the elemental influences which a person will pass through in his passage through life. Each luck pillar represents 10 years of influence. The small numbers marked on top of each luck pillar indicates the age at which a person will start coming under the influence of the luck pillar.

Supposing the example given in the previous appendix—10 a.m., 13 December 1993—is the birth data of a baby girl born at that moment. We can derive her luck pillar by just taking the month pillar (甲子) and moving both the heavenly stems and earthly branches forward by a space to obtain the first luck pillar. According to the table on page 14, the first luck pillar then becomes 乙丑. We can again move one space forward to the second luck pillar which is 丙寅, and repeat the procedure to find the third luck pillar and so on. We normally list out seven luck pillars as the life span of a person is around 70 years.

When listing out the luck pillars, it is important to distinguish between male and female, as the direction of movement of the luck pillar is different for men and women. The following rules apply:

Male born in yang year – move forward
Male born in yin year – move backward
Female born in yang year – move backward
Female born in yin year – move forward

Yang years mean singular or odd years; yin years mean plural or even years. For instance, 甲, the first heavenly stem, is yang and 乙, the second heavenly stem, is yin. By the same token, 子, the first earthly branch, is yang, and 丑, the second earthly branch, is yin.

In our example, as 1993, 癸酉, is a yin year, and this is a baby girl, the luck pillar moves forward. However, if it is a boy, a male born in a yin year, the luck pillars should move backward instead. Then the first luck pillar for the boy will be 癸亥, one space backward from the heavenly stem and earthly branch of the month pillar 甲子. The second luck pillar will be 壬戌, another space backward.

The last step is to enter the age at which each luck pillar takes effect. Three days in a month is considered a year of age. In our case, since the baby girl was born on 13 December 1993, the rule for setting up her luck pillar is to move forward. We should count the number of days forward until we reach the end of the month, which falls on 5 January 1994, as indicated by the black box in *The Thousand Years Almanac*. Between her birthday 13 December and 5 January, there are roughly 23 days. Twenty three divided by 3 roughly gives the result 8. This means that the baby girl will come under the influence of the first luck pillar 乙丑 at the age of 8. As each luck pillar will govern for about 10 years, she will be affected by the second luck pillar at the age of 18, the third luck pillar at the age of 28 and so on.

In the case of a baby boy born in 1993, the luck pillars will move backward. We count the number of days backward from the date of birth until we reach the starting date of the month. In our example, the previous black box showing the starting date of the month falls on 7 December.

There are roughly six days between 7 December and 13 December. As three days represent one year, dividing six by three gives us two years. So the boy will come under the influence of his first luck pillar 癸亥 at the age of two. The second luck pillar 壬戌 will start at the age of 12, the third luck pillar will commence at the age of 22, and so on. The following is the full set of Four Pillars of Destiny and luck pillars for the boy born at 10 a.m., 13 December 1993:

Hour	Day	Month	Year
丁	戊	甲	癸
Fire	Earth	Wood	Water
巳	辰	子	酉
Fire	Earth	Water	Metal

62	52	42	32	22	12	2
丁	戊	己	庚	辛	壬	癸
Fire	Earth	Earth	Metal	Metal	Water	Water
巳	午	未	申	酉	戌	亥
Fire	Fire	Earth	Metal	Metal	Earth	Water

If it is a baby girl, the luck pillar will move forward, starting at the age of 8, as described above.

APPENDIX 4

HOW TO FIND RELATIVES AND DIFFERENT ASPECTS OF LIFE FROM THE FOUR PILLARS OF DESTINY

1. To Find Relatives

Human relationships are symbolised in two ways in a set of Four Pillars of Destiny. They can be found by means of:

- Houses—the location in a set of Four Pillars of Destiny
- Stars—by the elemental relationship with the self as represented by the heavenly stem of the day pillar.

A. Houses:

HOUR	DAY	MONTH	YEAR
Son	Self	Father	Grandfather
Daughter	Spouse	Mother	Grandmother

For example, the heavenly stem of the month pillar always symbolises the father while the earthly branch of the month pillar symbolises the mother.

B. Stars:

As the heavenly stem of the day pillar represents the self, other relatives can be represented by other elements according to their relations with the self. The following are the rules for finding relatives, if the self is a male:

Mother – the element that gives birth to the self
Father – the element that is destroyed by the self
Offsprings – the element that destroys the self
Wife – the element that is destroyed by the self (same as the father)
Brothers/sisters – the element same as the self

What if the self is not male but female? The father, mother and brother/sisters can still be found the same way. However, the husband and the offsprings must be found differently.

Husband – the element that destroys the self
Offsprings – the element that the self gives birth to

The following, where the self is a wood man/wood woman, is an example:

	Self (wood man)	**Self (wood woman)**
Father	Earth	Earth
Mother	Water	Water
Wife	Earth	–
Husband	–	Metal
Offspring	Metal	Fire
Brother/sister	Wood	Wood

We can find other relationships according to the cycles of birth and destruction of the five elements. For example, if we want to find the father-in-law of the above wood man, the logic is that the father-in-law is the father of his wife. As his wife is earth, the father of an earth woman is the element that she destroys. So it is water that symbolises the father-in-law of the wood man.

When assessing the fortune of a relative from a set of Four Pillars of Destiny, we need to examine both the houses and the stars symbolising that relative. For example, to check the health of our father from our own set of Four Pillars of Destiny, examine the heavenly stem of the month pillar, as well as the element that is destroyed by the self. In our example of a wood man, this element is earth. If both are unfavourable the father could suffer from ill health.

2. To Find Different Aspects Of Life

The following cover the major aspects of life: Money, Power and Status, Authority and Resources, Aspiration and Intelligence, Colleagues and Friends. They can be found according to the elemental relationships to the self.

The rules to find these aspects are:

Money	– the element that the self destroys
Power and status	– the element that destroys the self
Authority and resources	– the element that gives birth to the self
Aspiration and intelligence	– the element that the self gives birth to
Colleagues, friends	– the element same as the self

For example, if the self is metal, the following represent his aspects of life:

Money	– Wood
Authority and resources	– Earth
Aspiration and intelligence	– Water
Power and status	– Fire
Colleagues, friends	– Metal

The following tables show the relationships and various aspects of life for persons of each of the five elements.

1. A METAL MAN

Element	**Persons**	**Areas of Life**
Metal	Self	Colleagues, competition
Earth	Mother	Resources, support, authority
Wood	Wife, father	Wealth, money
Fire	Son	Status, pressure, power
Water	–	Intelligence, expression

2. A WOOD MAN

Element	**Persons**	**Areas of Life**
Wood	Self	Colleagues, competition
Water	Mother	Resouces, support, authority
Earth	Wife, father	Wealth, money
Metal	Son	Status, pressure, power
Fire	–	Intelligence, expression

3. A WATER MAN

Element	**Persons**	**Areas of Life**
Water	Self	Colleagues, competition
Metal	Mother	Resouces, support, authority
Fire	Wife, father	Wealth, money
Earth	Son	Status, pressure, power
Wood	–	Intelligence, expression

4. A FIRE MAN

Element	Persons	Areas of Life
Fire	Self	Colleagues, competition
Wood	Mother	Resources, support, authority
Metal	Wife, father	Wealth, money
Water	Son	Status, pressure, power
Earth	–	Intelligence, expression

5. AN EARTH MAN

Element	Persons	Areas of Life
Earth	Self	Colleagues, competition
Fire	Mother	Resources, support, authority
Water	Wife, father	Wealth, money
Wood	Son	Status, pressure, power
Metal	–	Intelligence, expression

Note that a metal man is defined as a man with the heavenly stem of his day pillar belonging to the metal element. The same definition applies to the other four elements. The above table shows the relationships for a male. For a female, the only differences are the relations with the husband and the son. The following supplementary table lists the husband and son for all five types of females:

Self	Son	Husband
Metal woman	Water	Fire
Wood woman	Fire	Metal
Water woman	Wood	Earth
Fire woman	Earth	Water
Earth woman	Metal	Wood

The reasoning is that since a woman literally gives birth to her son, the element that is given birth by the self is the son. Ancient society also considered women the submissive sex to be conquered by the male. So the element that conquers the self is the husband. In all other aspects, the elemental relationships follow the patterns shown earlier.

APPENDIX 5

FIFTEEN STEPS TO DISCOVER YOUR DESTINY

1. Convert your birth data into the Four Pillars of Destiny by using *The Thousand Year Almanac*.
2. Add the heavenly stem to the hour pillar (See Appendix 2).
3. Derive the luck pillars from the month pillar.
   - Male yang year/female yin year—Forward
   - Male yin year/female yang year—Backward
4. Add the commencing age to the luck pillars.
   - Male yang year/female yin year—Count the number of days forward to reach the end of the month and divide by 3.
   - Male yin year/female yang year—Count the number of days backward to reach the beginning of the month and divide by 3.
5. Examine the day pillar. The heavenly stem of the day pillar represents the self. Establish the self element.
6. Establish the strength of the self element. Evaluate whether the self is strong or weak according to the season of birth and the quantity and quality of the supporting elements.
7. Determine the most favourable and unfavourable elements to the self.
8. Determine the second best and second worst elements to the self.
9. Establish the various aspects of life—power, wealth, authority, education, intelligence.
10. Establish the various human relationships—mother, father, friends, spouse, offspring.
11. Using the answers from steps 7 and 8, trace the luck pillars to see if your passage of life is smooth or full of obstacles.
12. Determine other aspects, such as career, health, character, mishaps, serious drawbacks and marriage.
13. Examine the current luck pillar. Is it a favourable element?
14. Examine the influence of the current year. Is it supportive or unfavourable?
15. Understand the nature of the current problem. Then advise.

APPENDIX 6

SEVENTEEN STEPS TO EVALUATE THE *FENG SHUI* OF A HOUSE

1. Determine the front and back of the building by inspecting its outlook and surroundings.
2. Measure the front direction with the Lo Pan.
3. Find out the Age of the building.
4. Draw up the relevant Flying Star chart.
5. Determine the prosperity of the building by comparing the physical surroundings with the chart. See if the mountain and water fit in well with the prosperous mountain stars and water stars.
6. Inspect the unit inside the building and sketch a floor plan.
7. Apply the Flying Star chart to the floor plan to see where the prosperous mountain stars and water stars of 7 and 8 affect the unit. Are the mountain stars placed on mountains (bedrooms)? Are the water stars placed in water (the living room, entrance, open spaces)?
8. Where are the bad stars of 2 and 5? Are they in vital positions such as bedrooms and entrances or are they in unimportant places such as toilets or storerooms.
9. Are there any physical drawbacks in the flat, such as sharp edges, dark corners or long and straight passageways.
10. What are the external circumstances of the flat? Are the good mountain stars of 7 and 8 supported by outside buildings? Are the water stars 7 and 8 supported by water or open spaces?
11. Are there any unique objects outside the window? (Physical shars)
12. Can any rearrangements be done? (From moving a bed to completely revising the interior design with changed partitions)
13. What are the current yearly and monthly influences at the front door and in the master bedroom?
14. Suggest objects to dissolve bad influences.
15. Measure the accurate dimensions of the flat.
16. Miscellaneous—any special history or happenings? Advise colour tones and special decorative objects.
17. Draw up the floor plan in scale, confirm the directions and Flying Stars influences and then make a full report.

APPENDIX 7

HOW TO DRAW UP A FLYING STAR CHART FOR A HOUSE

1. Determine the Age of the house and write the age number in the centre of a nine square chart. Then place the other eight numbers according to the Lo Shu pattern. The example below is an Age of Six building:

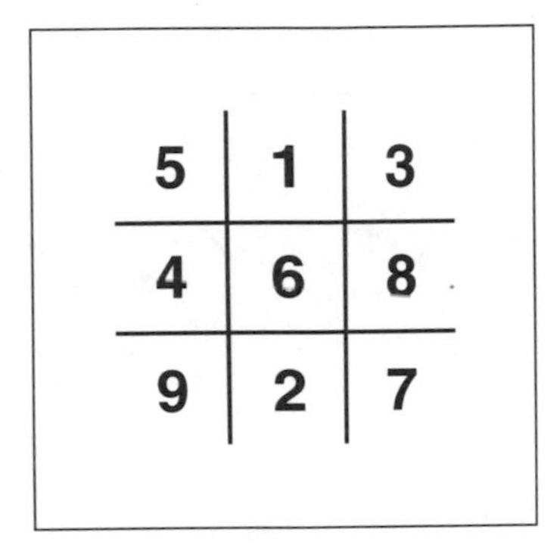

2. Determine the front and back direction of the house and enter the two numbers representing the two directions into the centre square. The back number is on the left while the front number on the right. For example, for an Age of Six building with its back against the east and the front facing west, the number 4 represents the east and the number 8 represents the west:

	5	1	3	
E	4	4 8 6	8	W
	9	2	7	

3. Determine the pattern of movement of the two middle numbers, either forward or backward, according to the following dial:

For example, if the measured direction of the above building is right east (back), right west (front), the characters in the Lo Pan are 卯 (Back) 酉 (Front). The two numbers entered in the centre of the nine square chart are 4 and 8.

From the dial, if you look up the number 4, you will find three 4s—4a, 4b and 4c—as there are 3 mountains to each direction. We select the middle one in this case, as the middle one means "right". However, if the measured direction is not "right east" but leaning towards NE, we have to select 4a. After selecting 4b, the F indicates it is a forward movement pattern. So you place the other numbers in ascending order in the other squares, in the ord r of 4, 5, 6, 7, 8, 9, 1, 2 and 3.

Now look up the number 8 in the dial. Select 8b. The indication is F, sc the movement is in ascending order of 8, 9, 1, 2, 3, 4, 5, 6 and 7. If you see B, the movement is backward and descending, so you should count 8, 7, 6, 5, 4, 3, 2, 1 and 9.

Flying star chart for an Age of Six house facing exact west

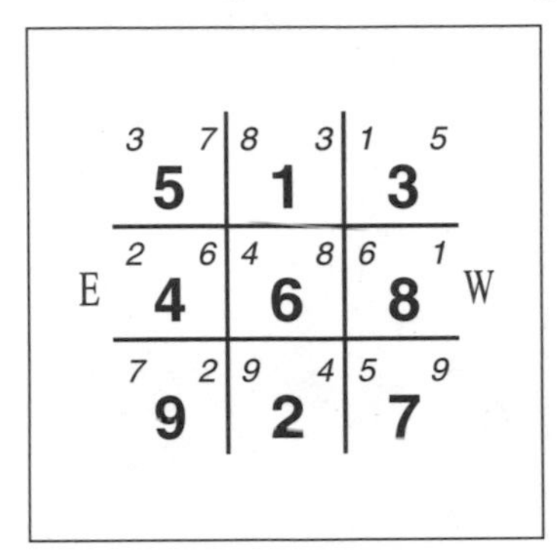

4. What if the centre small number is 5? You will not be able to find a 5 on the dial. Instead, the Age number should be used to determine the forward or backward movement of the 5. For example, if it is a SE - NW house of Age of Six, but leaning to E-W, the 5 in the SE goes to the centre. Then you should look up 6a in the diagram where the indication is B. So the movement should be backward and descending, that is, 5, 4, 3, 2, 1, 9, 8, 7 and 6.

Flying star chart for an Age of Six house facing northwest

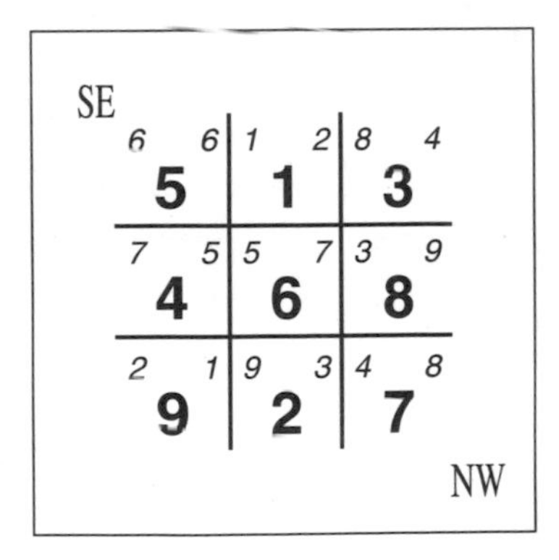

APPENDIX 8

THE FLYING STAR CHARTS AND ESSENTIAL SHARS (1992–2009)

	S	
7	3 (3 shars)	5 (year star)
6	8	1
2 (clash star)	4	9

1992

	S	
6	2	4
(clash star) 5 (3 shars)	7	(year star) 9
1	3	8

1993

	S	
(clash star) 5	1	3
4	6	8
9	(3 shars) 2	(year star) 7

1994

	S	
(clash star) 4	9	2
3	5	(3 shars) 7
8	1	(year star) 6

1995

	S	
3	(clash star) 8 (3 shars)	1
2	4	6
7	(year star) 9	5

1996

	S	
2	7	(clash star) 9
(3 shars) 1	3	5
6 (year star)	8	4

1997

	S	
1	6	8 clash star
9	2	4
5 year star	7 3 shars	3

1998

	S	
9	5	7
8 year star	1	3 shars 3 clash star
4	6	2

1999

	S	
8 year star	4 3 shars	6
7	9	2
3	5	1 clash star

2000

	S	
7 year star	3	5
6 3 shars	8	1
2	4	9 clash star

2001

	S	
6	2 year star	4
5	7	9
1	3 shars 3 clash star	8

2002

	S	
5	1	3 year star
4	6	8 3 shars
9 clash star	2	7

2003

	S	
4	9 3 shars	2 year star
3	5	7
8 clash star	1	6

2004

	S	
3	8	1
3 shars 2 clash star	4	6 year star
7	9	5

2005

	S	
2 clash star	7	9
1	3	5
6	8 3 shars	4 year star

2006

	S	
1 clash star	6	8
9	2	4 3 shars
5	7	3 year star

2007

	S	
9	3 shars 5 clash star	7
8	1	3
4	6 year star	2

2008

	S	
8	4	6 clash star
7 3 shars	9	2
3 year star	5	1

2009

APPENDIX 9

GUIDE TO LABELLING HEXAGRAMS FOR THE I CHING ORACLE

1. Toss your three coins six times to obtain your hexagram as described in the chapter *How To Perform An I Ching Oracle*.
2. Draw your hexagram in continuous and broken lines according to the configuration of the coins. Find the same hexagram in the index table and the corresponding index number for the hexagram.
   For example, if the hexagram you have obtained is:

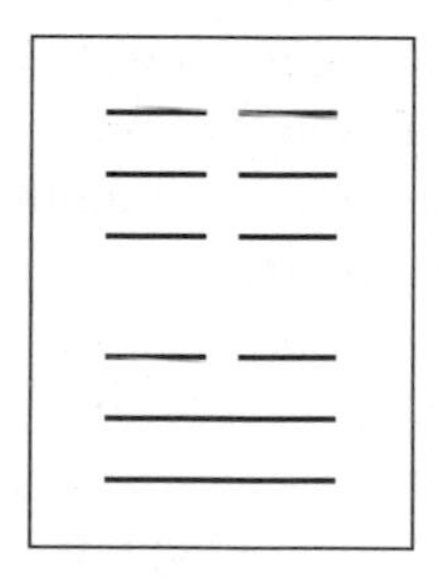

   The index table identifies it as 2c.
3. Look up the following pages and find the relevant hexagram 2c with labels. You should obtain the fully labeled hexagram as follows:

Metal — —
Water — — O
Earth — —

Earth — —
Wood ——— S
Fire ———

The letter "S" means subject line while "O" stands for object line. As a rule, they are always two lines apart.

The kua element is found at the top of the page. In our example, the kua element is earth. This is used for further labelling the hexagram to find the various aspects of life as described on page 132. You can thus label the various aspects of hexagram 2c as follows:

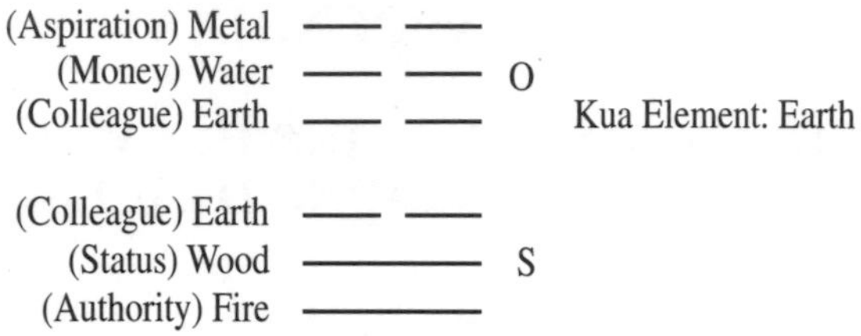

```
(Aspiration) Metal  —— ——
    (Money) Water   —— ——   O
(Colleague) Earth   —— ——        Kua Element: Earth

(Colleague) Earth   —— ——
    (Status) Wood   ———————   S
(Authority) Fire    ———————
```

The kua numbers are also indicated at the top of each page. The kua number is named after the Lo Shu diagram and is used here to identify each Trigram of the I Ching. Observe that the number 5 is missing. This is because the 5 is in the centre of the Lo Shu diagram and does not represent a Trigram. You can refer to page 66 for more information about the Lo Shu diagram.

4. In many cases, you will encounter active lines. Active lines mean yang changes to yin or vice versa. In our example, let us assume that the fourth line from the bottom is an active line, changing from yin to yang. You can then add a yang line beside the fourth line.

You need to label this active line. The first step is to look up the index table to find the hexagram with the fourth line changed to yang and identify its number. In our example, the hexagram is numbered 7h. Now find hexagram 7h in the following pages and check the element label for the fourth line. Write down the element (fire) for the active line. Find the aspects by comparing this element with the original kua element, which is earth in our example. As fire is the mother of earth, label this active line "Authority".

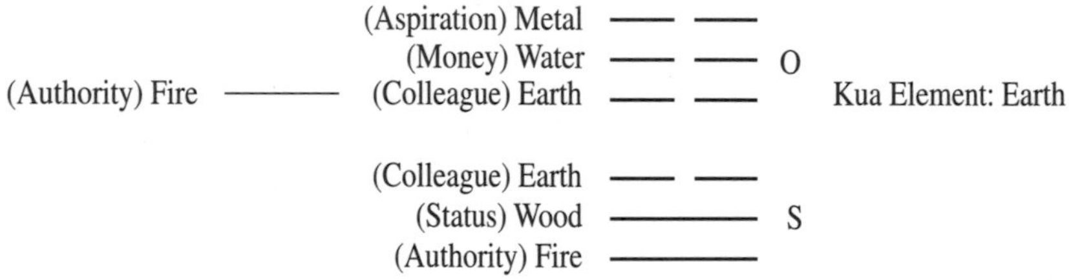

```
                                (Aspiration) Metal  —— ——
                                    (Money) Water   —— ——   O
(Authority) Fire  ———————      (Colleague) Earth   —— ——        Kua Element: Earth

                                (Colleague) Earth   —— ——
                                    (Status) Wood   ———————   S
                                (Authority) Fire    ———————
```

5. The figure above shows a fully labelled hexagram. You can now begin your interpretation.

Index for the 64 hexagrams

9	8	7	6	4	3	2	1	
								A
								B
								C
								D
								E
								F
								G
								H

— —
———
— —

Kua Element: Water

Kua Number: 1

A.
Water — — S
Earth ———
Metal — —

Fire — — O
Earth ———
Wood — —

B.
Water — —
Earth ———
Metal — — O

Earth — —
Wood ———
Fire ——— S

C.
Water — —
Earth ———
Metal — — O

Earth — —
Wood — — S
Water ———

D.
Water — — O
Earth ———
Metal — —

Water ——— S
Earth — —
Wood ———

E.
Earth — —
Metal ———
Water ——— S

Water ———
Earth — —
Wood ——— O

F.
Earth — —
Metal — — S
Fire ———

Water ———
Earth — — O
Wood ———

G.
Metal — —
Water — —
Earth — — S

Water ———
Earth — —
Wood ——— O

H.
Metal — — O
Water — —
Earth — —

Fire — — S
Earth ———
Wood — —

— —
— —
— —

Kua Element: Earth

Kua Number: 2

A.
Metal — — S
Water — —
Earth — —

Wood — — O
Fire — —
Earth — —

B.
Metal — —
Water — —
Earth — — O

Earth — —
Wood — —
Water ——— S

C.
Metal — —
Water — — O
Earth — —

Earth — —
Wood ——— S
Fire ———

D.
Metal — — O
Water — —
Earth — —

Earth ——— S
Wood ———
Water ———

E.
Earth — —
Metal — —
Fire ——— S

Earth ———
Wood ———
Water ——— O

F.
Earth — —
Metal ——— S
Water ———

Earth ———
Wood ——— O
Water ———

G.
Water — —
Earth ———
Metal — — S

Earth ———
Wood ———
Water ——— O

H.
Water — — O
Earth ———
Metal — —

Wood — — S
Fire — —
Earth — —

— — Kua Element: Wood
— —
——— Kua Number: 3

A. Earth — — S
Metal — —
Fire ———

Earth — — O
Wood — —
Water ———

B. Earth — —
Metal — —
Fire ——— O

Wood — —
Fire — —
Earth — — S

C. Earth — —
Metal — — O
Fire ———

Fire — —
Earth ——— S
Wood — —

D. Earth — — O
Metal — —
Fire ———

Metal ——— S
Water ———
Earth — —

E. Metal — —
Water — —
Earth — — S

Metal ———
Water ———
Earth — — O

F. Water — —
Earth ——— S
Metal — —

Metal ———
Water ——— O
Earth — —

G. Earth — —
Metal ———
Water ——— S

Metal ———
Water ———
Earth — — O

H. Earth — — O
Metal ———
Water ———

Earth — — S
Wood — —
Water ———

——— Kua Element: Wood
———
— — Kua Number: 4

A. Wood ——— S
Fire ———
Earth — —

Metal ——— O
Water ———
Earth — —

B. Wood ———
Fire ———
Earth — — O

Earth ———
Wood ———
Water ——— S

C. Wood ———
Fire ——— O
Earth — —

Water ———
Earth — — S
Wood ———

D. Wood ——— O
Fire ———
Earth — —

Earth — — S
Wood — —
Water ———

E. Earth ———
Metal ———
Fire ——— S

Earth — —
Wood — —
Water ——— O

F. Fire ———
Earth — — S
Metal ———

Earth — —
Wood — — O
Water ———

G. Wood ———
Water — —
Earth — — S

Earth — —
Wood — —
Water ——— O

H. Wood ——— O
Water — —
Earth — —

Metal ——— S
Water ———
Earth — —

———
———
———

Kua Element: Metal

Kua Number: 6

A.	B.	C.	D.
Earth ——— S	Earth ———	Earth ———	Earth ——— O
Metal ———	Metal ———	Metal ——— O	Metal ———
Fire ———	Fire ——— O	Fire ———	Fire ———
Earth ——— O	Metal ———	Metal ———	Wood — — S
Wood ———	water ———	Fire — — S	Fire — —
Water ———	Earth — — S	Earth — —	Earth — —

E.	F.	G.	H.
Wood ———	Wood ———	Fire ———	Fire ——— O
Fire ———	Water — — S	Earth — —	Earth — —
Earth — — S	Earth — —	Metal ——— S	Metal ———
Wood — —	Wood — —	Wood — —	Earth ——— S
Fire — —	Fire — — O	Fire — —	Wood ———
Earth — — O	Earth — —	Earth — — O	Water ———

— —
———
———

Kua Element: Metal

Kua Number: 7

A.	B.	C.	D.
Earth — — S	Earth — —	Earth — —	Earth — — O
Metal ———	Metal ———	Metal ——— O	Metal ———
Water ———	Water ——— O	Water ———	Water ———
Earth — — O	Fire — —	Wood — —	Metal ——— S
Wood ———	Earth ———	Fire — — S	Fire — —
Fire ———	Wood — — S	Earth — —	Earth — —

E.	F.	G.	H.
Water — —	Metal — —	Earth — —	Earth — — O
Earth ———	Water — — S	Metal — —	Metal — —
Metal — — S	Earth — —	Fire ——— S	Fire ———
Metal ———	Metal ———	Metal ———	Earth — — S
Fire — —	Fire — — O	Fire — —	Wood ———
Earth — — O	Earth — —	Earth — — O	Fire ———

———
— —
— —

Kua Element: Earth

Kua Number: 8

A.			**B.**			**C.**			**D.**		
Wood	———	S	Wood	———		Wood	———		Wood	———	O
Water	— —		Water	— —		Water	— —	O	Water	— —	
Earth	— —		Earth	— —	O	Earth	— —		Earth	— —	
Metal	———	O	Water	———		Earth	———		Earth	— —	S
Fire	— —		Earth	— —		Wood	———	S	Wood	———	
Earth	— —		Wood	———	S	Water	———		Fire	———	

E.			**F.**			**G.**			**H.**		
Fire	———		Earth	———		Wood	———		Wood	———	O
Earth	— —		Metal	———	S	Fire	———		Fire	———	
Metal	———	S	Fire	———		Earth	— —	S	Earth	— —	
Earth	— —		Earth	— —		Earth	— —		Metal	———	S
Wood	———		Wood	———	O	Wood	———		Fire	— —	
Fire	———	O	Fire	———		Fire	———	O	Earth	— —	

———
— —
———

Kua Element: Fire

Kua Number: 9

A.			**B.**			**C.**			**D.**		
Fire	———	S	Fire	———		Fire	———		Fire	———	O
Earth	— —		Earth	— —		Earth	— —	O	Earth	— —	
Metal	———		Metal	———	O	Metal	———		Metal	———	
Water	———	O	Metal	———		Metal	———		Fire	— —	S
Earth	— —		Fire	— —		Water	———	S	Earth	———	
Wood	———		Earth	— —	S	Earth	— —		Wood	— —	

E.			**F.**			**G.**			**H.**		
Wood	———		Wood	———		Earth	———		Earth	———	O
Water	— —		Fire	———	S	Metal	———		Metal	———	
Earth	— —	S	Earth	— —		Fire	———	S	Fire	———	
Fire	— —		Fire	— —		Fire	— —		Water	———	S
Earth	———		Earth	———	O	Earth	———		Earth	— —	
Wood	— —	O	Wood	— —		Wood	— —	O	Wood	———	

The Author

Raymond Lo, popularly known as "*Feng Shui Lo*" in Hong Kong, is a professional *feng shui* researcher and practitioner. His experience also covers the Four Pillars of Destiny and the predictions of the I Ching Oracle.

After graduating with a degree in Social Sciences from the University of Hong Kong, Mr. Lo's interest in *feng shui* led him to seriously study the ancient art. He subsequently learnt to explain the complicated theories of Chinese metaphysics in a concise and logical manner, using this skill to write a popular *feng shui* column in *The Hong Kong Standard* between 1988 and 1991. In this column he made several forecasts about world events, including the outbreak and the result of the Gulf War, the fall of Mikhail Gorbachev and Margaret Thatcher's resignation, all of which later proved to be accurate.

Mr. Lo is the author of *Feng Shui: The Pillars of Destiny* and has published several other *feng shui* titles in Chinese. He frequently contributes his knowledge of *feng shui* to various media publications. In 1990, he made a "live" appearance on the popular BBC programme *Whicker's World*. In 1994, he introduced *feng shui* to American audiences in the ABC programme *Good Morning America*. He is also a *feng shui* lecturer at the School of Professional and Continual Education in the University of Hong Kong.